llenging concep... it

as this selection of posters

and uniqueness are impor-

y other ge...ters are

d often widely distributed.

ultiple, briefly seeming to

ll their many-faceted vari-

rriding requirement – they

his effectiveness arises from

ds, symbols, and design.

POSTERS AMERICAN STYLE

Posters American Style

Therese Thau Heyman

National Museum of American Art, Smithsonian Institution

in association with

Harry N. Abrams, Inc., Publishers

CONT

FOREWORD   6

Elizabeth Broun, Director,
National Museum of American Art,
Smithsonian Institution

ACKNOWLEDGMENTS   9

POSTERS AMERICAN STYLE   12

Therese Thau Heyman, Guest Curator,
National Museum of American Art

GUIDE TO POSTERMAKING TERMS   33

PLATES

American Events   34
Designed to Sell   68
Patriots and Protestors   96
Advice for Americans   124
Sports   150

ENTS

BIOGRAPHIES OF   158
THE POSTERMAKERS

BIBLIOGRAPHY   178

CHRONOLOGICAL INDEX   185

INDEX   188

PHOTOGRAPH CREDITS   191

Foreword

Posters American Style, which accompanies a touring exhibition of the same name, brings together some of the great graphic images made in the United States over the past century. Posters have been exhibited and published occasionally by the National Museum of American Art but not previously collected at the Museum as an essential chapter in the story of our nation's visual culture. This book and show, and the fledgling collection now begun, signal the Museum's new awareness of the vital role played by these high-keyed and exciting images.

For many decades, this first federal art museum was a traditional painting and sculpture gallery following the European model. When fine prints and drawings began entering the collections years ago, those allied with commercial purposes or processes were excluded. Over the past quarter century, however, the appreciation of our own idiomatic expressions has grown to include many art forms and traditions previously omitted. In 1972, the Museum inaugurated a major program for crafts in the Renwick Gallery, inspiring exhibitions ranging from Tiffany glass to wicker furniture and modern studio crafts. A decade later, an ambitious photography program began, quickly growing to span the whole history of the medium. In 1986 and 1997, the Museum acquired major collections of works by self-taught artists that fit no conventional category of art, requiring a new set of "first principles" to be understood.

Each time the Museum's program expands into another neglected area, a current of energy flows through the overall program. New artists emerge as significant figures and new aspects of experience find a voice. Cross-references between collections challenge old assumptions and reinforce other ideas about how we have pictured ourselves for more than two hundred years.

Posters American Style is invaluable for showing an exuberant, persuasive, even argumentative side to American culture that would seem out of place in the more refined arts of painting and sculpture. Posters capture us bargaining in the marketplace, protesting in the city square, flagging down passersby, or just letting off steam. Our highest ideals may inspire posters as readily as paintings, but those ideals will be presented more frankly, with biting wit, hilarious humor, or shocking imagery. Posters don't hold back.

Americans have been making powerful posters for the past one hundred years, since advances in printing made possible large-format, full-color pictures in big, cheap editions. They seem at first like a simple, direct kind of art making, but a closer look shows how they imaginatively integrate commerce and art, propaganda and protest, image and message, mass technology and personal expression. Postermaking grew up as a tool of advertising, communications, and marketing by targeting large audiences with common experience. The sheer number of posters designed and distributed over the past century is daunting, touching on almost every subject and presenting one index of our concerns and interests.

Any selection from the many thousands of surviving posters must necessarily be incomplete and subjective; however, curator Therese Heyman has focused this gathering on major artists and images that have endured in our collective memory. Combing through private and public collections across the country, she has winnowed a wealth of material, highlighting the finest designers and most urgent messages while documenting movements and revivals that establish a historical overview. She has focused on key issues, including many points of view. For instance, the small selection from the enormous category of war-related posters runs the gamut from exhortations to the home front to anti-war dissent.

Although we think of posters as a well-known popular art, in fact the sheer difficulty of handling and framing oversize fragile sheets of paper means that most collections remain hidden in the drawers of museum map-cases, rarely seen by the public they were made to reach. Exhibitions that cut across subject categories are especially rare, since collections were usually formed around themes – bicycle advertisements, circus or movie posters, war images, rock music – which make natural groupings for exhibitions, obviating the need to sift whole collections for just one or two images.

Still fewer exhibitions and books have focused on posters as a manifestation of American experience, though the subject is rich. This selection reveals how posters accomplish their work of transforming our visual culture while promoting a particular event, product, or idea. Early circus and advertising posters remain favorites today because they present flamboyant images that coax us to linger, invoking a world of leisure and entertainment. Barnum & Bailey's baseball-playing elephants belie the conventional wisdom that posters are meant for a short attention span. These arresting early posters debuted in an image-poor world, when advertisements were confined to small black-and-white illustrations and political protest made do with simple broadsides. The exuberance of early poster designs, filling every inch with abundant imagery and trans-forming text into a brilliant display, shows how artists were inspired by new processes that could inexpensively produce very large, colorful images.

The trend toward a simpler, more direct, and forceful poster image developed over the early decades of the twentieth century, as posters competed for attention in an expanding visual field. *I Want You for U.S. Army* signaled a new appreciation for a concentrated image, an immediately recognizable symbol, and terse text. We are transfixed by this hypnotic icon, almost unable to turn our gaze away from the head-on confrontation. Image and text are distilled to their essence, readable at a glance and assimilable on the deepest levels. A half century after they were made, Norman Rockwell's *Four Freedoms* still represent to us America's best ideals, however much we debate whether these freedoms have been successfully achieved. Such commanding images are favorites of government and industry, for they speak from a position of authority and aim to unite us in a common cause.

Another kind of poster relies on a subversive twist, a disjunction between image and message that gives vital expression to dissent. *Sun Mad Raisins*, produced for the farmworkers' movement, cleverly turns a well-known ad campaign into environmental protest. The first casual glance produces instant recognition of a familiar image, but a closer look turns it upside down. Visual and verbal puns upset our expectations. Such "one-two punch" posters, introduced in the mid-twentieth century, depend on a visually sophisticated audience used to a daily bombardment of images in many media. We tune out much of what we see or note it quickly in passing, and our momentary lapse in attention gives postermakers an opening that they often exploit with surprising effect.

Is there something essentially American in the art of postermaking? While many societies have produced great posters, it does seem that there is a fundamentally democratic quality to the communication strategies of posters. American expression in all media – music, performance, literature, visual arts – has been fertilized by vernacular culture on the one hand and by industry and commerce on the other. While fine art in America took cues from European styles valued by high society, popular art forms fed on the renewable energy of daily experience. For decades in early America, shared visual imagery was mainly religious or federal in nature, but new photographic and printing processes developed during the Industrial Revolution created an imagery rooted in personal experience. Just as free speech guarantees expression for evolving political beliefs, the infinite possibilities of popular culture allow us to adapt to an ever-changing society.

Posters are classified as "ephemera," which means that they are intended to be used – and to affect their audience – for only a short time. But their fundamental connection to so many specific moments helps us track our history from the ground-level view of daily life. Today, as website designers seek vibrant graphic images and powerful, terse captions to appeal to mass audiences, the fundamental lessons of poster design seem more contemporary than ever. And as telecommunications technologies promise a new democratization of publishing in years to come, this sampling of great posters offers one of the best records available of our aspirations, concerns, and struggles in the "American Century" now concluding.

The National Museum of American Art is grateful to Therese Thau Heyman, guest curator, for editing this book and curating the accompanying exhibition. We also thank Peter and Helen Bing for their generous support of the project, and the Smithsonian's Special Exhibitions Program for additional assistance.

ELIZABETH BROUN
Director, National Museum of American Art

Acknowledgments

Many of us select posters for our rooms, a few of us become collectors, and together with many museum visitors, we look forward to the occasional poster exhibition. Most recent shows have focused on specific poster themes – World War I designs for government agencies, the home front during World War II, contemporary European-style graphics, and highlights of 1890s literary poster collections – but no recent exhibition before this one has attempted a survey of the major contributions of American posters. This very large undertaking, involving both well-recognized postermakers and others who are virtually unknown in that field, today depends on the help and interest of many generous people who assisted me in my search through bits of mostly unrelated information. For biographical material and leads to the obscure, I am indebted to many researchers, collectors, and galleries as well as the major institutions that hold the largest collections.

Finding a source of financial support that would ensure the realization of the exhibition and this catalogue was a lengthy task. Fortunately for the National Museum of American Art, one advocate for posters responded favorably, directly, and generously to our proposal. Helen Bing, who has installed poster collections in various institutions, is aware of the power of posters. She and Dr. Peter Bing are the major sponsors of the educational aspects of the exhibition and this book. It is a pleasure for me to have the opportunity to continue our friendship through our shared interest in this project.

A select group of scholars with a passion for posters have shared their ideas and suggestions with me. I have been fortunate that three leading experts were close by in Washington, where we could meet to discuss the challenges of this hundred-year survey. My special thanks go to Neil Harris, Preston and Sterling Morton professor of History, University of Chicago, whose important, well-documented, and delightfully written article on collecting posters appears in the spring 1998 issue of *American Art*.

Alan Fern has made time in his busy schedule as director of the National Portrait Gallery to discuss the many ways that a poster survey could cut through the available wealth of images, an area he has come to know well from his prior experience as curator of the prints and photograph collections at the Library of Congress. Bernard Reilly, also a former curator of prints and photographs at the library, now Director of Research and Access at the Chicago Historical Society, proposed valuable sources.

The biographical information located by Smithsonian interns Leo Costello, Julie Charles, and Anne Samuels immeasurably aided my search for more than eighty postermakers and their works. While many of the postermakers were well known in the other areas of the arts, their posters were relatively unfamiliar. Interns David Archangeli, Carolyn Bastian, Erica Davis, Danielle Raymond and Rebekah Rotstein discovered many new accounts of these somewhat obscure commissions.

Galleries and collectors have answered my questions and often further supported the exhibition with notable gifts of posters. I would like to thank Barry and Melissa Vilkin; Tomás Ybarra-Frausto, who presented us with special collections; Todd Padgett at Louvre of San Francisco; Nancy McLaughlin at the National Parks publication office; Angel Broadnax at the Bureau of the Census; and Tom Oxendine, retired from the Bureau of Indian Affairs.

A great variety of hands – photographer, printer, publisher, and designer – cooperate in the creation of posters. I am grateful to Julie Charles, who began the research on this complex collaboration, Jeana Foley, who continued this aspect of the research, and others with remarkable organizational skills, dedication, and tenacity. At a time when my notes on the more than 120 posters were in need of careful source checking, I was fortunate to have the skillful assistance of Alison Dineen, who brought order to the many entries. Again, I have turned to the experienced and patient editor Lorna Price for reviewing and suggesting changes to numerous versions of the text.

For leads on the little-known stories about specific posters, I want to thank many lenders who are willing and learned scholars for their own collections. Among them are Gary Ruttenberg, Elliot Stanley, Merrill Berman, Mary Haskell, and Steven Schmidt.

One of the pleasures of working with contemporary postermakers is the opportunity to learn firsthand about choices they make in creating a particular image as well as the process they adopted to create the edition. Indeed, in poster printing, often only the postermaker and publisher can supply such details. Art Chantry, Seymour Chwast, Ivan Chermayeff, Rupert García, Milton Glaser, April Greiman, David Lance Goines, Ester Hernandez, Frank Kozik, and Wes Wilson contributed invaluable information. I am deeply thankful that at a

particularly fortunate moment in the late 1960s I interviewed Bill Graham, then the young concert producer at Fillmore Auditorium, about the surprisingly popular posters being made under his direction.

Many devoted gallery owners and dealers introduced me to new works. I extend my thanks for their helpful suggestions to Jack Banning and Louis Bixenman at PosterAmerica; Jack Rennert of Posters Please and Poster Auctions International; Todd Padgett of Louvre, San Francisco; Richard Solomon, Pace Prints; and Felice Regan of The Graphic Workshop.

I am especially grateful to the many lenders who made special arrangements for me to see posters, including Frances S. Balter of the Poetry on the Buses Project, Moreton Binn and Jonathan Binstock for Peter Max, Merrill Berman at his extensive collection, and Mary Haskell, Leonard Lauder, Stanley Picheny, Gary Ruttenberg, and Leslie Schreyer.

As oversized posters on fragile paper defy most storage systems, my colleagues in other museums often made special arrangements for me to view posters at a location off-site. Kristin L. Spangenberg of the Cincinnati Art Museum; Elaina S. Danielson of the Hoover Institution on War, Revolution, and Peace; Jay Fisher of The Baltimore Museum of Art; Charles Moffett of The Phillips Collection; Sidney Lawrence of the Hirshhorn Museum and Sculpture Garden; Alan Fern and Wendy Reaves of the National Portrait Gallery; W. Robert Johnston of the National Museum of American Art; Gianna Capecci of the Oakland Museum; Sinclaire Hitchings of The Boston Public Library; Ellen Lupton and Marilyn Symmes at the Cooper-Hewitt; Mary F. Houlahan of the Delaware Art Museum; Annette Fern at the Harvard Theater Collection; Elena Millie of the Library of Congress; Stacey Bredhoff and Nick Natanson at the National Archives; Kathryn Henderson, Harry Rubenstein, and Craig A. Orr at the National Museum of American History; Jerry Pompili of Bill Graham

Presents; George Goldner of The Metropolitan Museum of Art; Dennis Love of the Pacific Film Archives; and Frederick Brandt of the Virginia Museum of Fine Arts.

This book and exhibition could not exist at the Smithsonian without the enthusiastic and continuing support of Elizabeth Broun, who, as Director of the National Museum of American Art, has fostered this extensive undertaking in all its phases with her knowledgeable advice. I have been fortunate as a guest curator to have the enthusiastic support of all the staff who have anticipated the need to teach me the Museum's special systems. A show of this complexity involves all departments of the Museum, and I want to thank Virginia Mecklenburg and Jacquelyn Serwer for their expert advice. I am fortunate to have the experienced help of Charles Robertson, Deputy Director, who arranged for the generous contribution from the Special Exhibition Funds of the Smithsonian.

I am grateful to the registrars Melissa Kroning, Patti Hager, and Michael Smallwood for their many suggestions on the loans, tour, and permissions. Happily, there are many staff members who them-selves collect posters, and I thank Robyn Kennedy in Design and Production and Robert Johnston in External Affairs for loans. Among the curators, Joann Moser unfailingly aided my ideas about acquisitions; additional knowledge and discoveries were brought to light by Lynn Putney, Denise Dougherty, and Marjorie Zapruder. Design and installation were ably planned by John Zelenik, Martin Kotler, and Charles Booth. The complex task of editing and combining texts for this book, the exhibition, and the World Wide Web site was cheerfully and patiently provided by Theresa Slowik, Janet Wilson, and Steve Bell.

My thanks go to the staff at Abrams led by Margaret Kaplan, Margaret Braver, and Ellen Nygaard Ford.

To my husband, Michael, once again my thanks for accompanying me to visit many out-of-the-way galleries and collections as well as for his support for a large project completed in a short time.

THERESE THAU HEYMAN
Guest Curator

Posters American Style

Therese Thau Heyman

At the present time, poster art is in a period of renaissance. Posters have come to be regarded as mysterious cultural objects, whose flatness and literalness only deepen their resonance, as well as inexhaustibly rich emblems of the society. . . . Posters have become one of the most ubiquitous kinds of cultural objects – prized partly because they are cheap, unpretentious, "popular" art.[1]

– Susan Sontag

The purpose of American posters has always been to grab the individual and the collective consciousness and demand attention. Whatever the message – from patriotic appeals to voices raised in protest, from pleas for environmentalism to seductive suggestions urging us to buy jeans – the poster reflects the explosion of ideas in the twentieth century, both intellectual and visual. Designers adapt quickly to changes in the social landscape to keep their posters a fresh and vital means of communication.

Through the broad scope of *Posters American Style* we explore the strategies of commerce, propaganda, and patriotism. While it is not possible to trace all the many changes in poster styles in the last one hundred years, it is evident that to attract attention poster artists must constantly search for a fresh approach and an element of the unexpected. Despite conventional wisdom that the straightforward solution may be the clearest communication, it may also be so dull that the message is never read.[2]

From the outset, American posters have benefited from embracing the gaudy as well as the refined, the blatant as well as the subtle. The 120 posters depicted here include distinctively American elements that have contributed to the medium in terms of design, text, and image – among them the circus, the literary magazine, the Works Progress Administration's multifaceted projects, the psychedelic performance. Recent trends in poster design range from modernist approaches to those intended to appeal as mass media.

J. Howard Miller, Westinghouse for War Production Coordinating Committee. *We Can Do It!* (detail). See plate 68.

This survey views the American poster through its early examples, its peculiar slogans, and its visual devices, which incorporate a diverse vocabulary of symbols that have broad appeal for Americans. Each poster campaign has considered its targeted audience, from aesthetes to peaceniks; despite the resulting diversity, a vocabulary of visual symbols emerges, and a uniquely American accent prevails.

American style is a challenging concept, and it may have many meanings, as this selection of posters demonstrates. While rarity and uniqueness are important considerations in many other genres, posters are by definition numerous and often widely distributed. They reach out; they are multiple, briefly seeming to appear everywhere. Yet in all their many-faceted variety, they fulfill the one overriding requirement – they communicate effectively. This effectiveness arises from a complex layering of words, symbols, and design.

In American circus posters created in the first decades of the twentieth century, for instance, the acts staged in the big top provided the poster's visual content – a crowded assembly of animals, freaks, and high-wire acrobats appear in the Strobridge posters[3] – as well as informative text about the date, time, owner, and publisher, in brilliant, eye-catching colors (plates 1, 2, 3).

Slogans distinguish many posters. In Ben Shahn's *A Good Man Is Hard to Find,* we read a phrase familiar as a song and also as a political slogan, which reminds us that this poster supports Henry Wallace's 1948 campaign (plate 72). Adding to the political commentary, this poster offers a visible moral jab with another song title, "Little White Lies." The slogans, available to a mass audience, combined with the work of an experienced graphic artist and postermaker, allowed the brief phrase to convey complex messages.

Often, just one word can get the message across by building on a broadly shared social imperative. In both world wars, "Enlist" came as a command, which was often the poster's message and purpose. Such shorthand requires an easily shared idiom, as in the famous slogan "I Want You for U.S. Army" (plate 60).

Many American posters capitalize on a specific group's interests and perhaps its sense of identity. Such posters address a targeted audience and simultaneously inform the majority. Today they may also be intended to give an effective voice to a culture. Through images reminiscent of Mexican murals, of folk art, and through portraits of revered figures such as Frida Kahlo, Rupert García engages a Chicano audience. For an exhibition of Mexican and Chicano art at The Mexican Museum in San Francisco, García printed woodblock-style posters in the brilliant color and vitality associated with Chicano design (plate 23). In another poster, he offers a pointed and persuasive

Ben Shahn, The Progressive Party (New York). *A Good Man Is Hard to Find* (detail depicting Truman and Dewey). See plate 72.

message against stereotypes in advertising by subverting the familiar image of a smiling black chef delivering a bowl of cereal with a new text: "No More o' This Shit" (plate 83).

Posters communicate, invite action, build consensus. Fred Spear's 1915 drawing of a drowning mother and child (plate 59) was directly adapted from a tabloid newspaper account of the fate of the *Lusitania,* the civilian passenger ship sunk by a German submarine in the North Sea: "On the Cunard wharf lies a mother with a three-month-old child clasped tightly in her arms. Her face wears a half smile. Her baby's head rests against her breast. No one has tried to separate them."[4]

The poster translates this news report into an evocative image, pulling the audience into the event. At the same moment, by pointing to the tragedy, the poster elicits an urgent response. Motherhood, loss of life, and revenge suggest a single action: "Enlist."

Because so many posters exist, our selection process was stringent. First, the work had to be a design developed specifically for a poster and not simply a work of art transferred from another medium. Museum and exhibition posters, for example, typically include a reproduction of an artwork that will be in the show. Though appealing, such works are not wholly original poster designs in which the elements of type, image, and composition come together to complete a new communication.

As a consequence of the growing interest in literary magazines in the 1890s, posters were designed to encourage even more subscribers. William H. Bradley, one of the most influential postermakers of that decade, commented on his work in a letter:

> *My first decorative poster was done for Harper & Brothers for their* April Magazine, *1893. It was done only as an experiment and [it] was some long time before I heard of Lautrec or Steinlen as poster designers. . . . Later on, Richard Harding asked me to make a poster for his book* Our English Cousins *and showed me about a dozen French posters which were the first I had ever seen. I think the American Poster has opened a new school whose aim is simplicity and good composition. One can see its effect in all directions, especially in the daily papers.*[5]

Bradley, a trained printer and engraver, started his own firm in Springfield, Massachusetts, in 1895, producing such books as *Bradley: His Chap-Book,* and many fine composed works, including posters for local firms. Most were for safely acceptable products such as bicycles, but *Narcoti-Cure* (plate 33) seems suspect. Here the

Fred Spear. *Enlist* (detail). See plate 59.

familiar style of children's book illustration makes a disturbing contrast to the nature of the chemical company's promise. Bradley's commercial posters reflect his success in using fine art to forward business objectives.[6] The tension between the fine art of design and the commercial needs of advertising, between the artist and the client, continues to challenge postermakers.

THE ALPHABET AND ROCK 'N' ROLL

While there seemed to be general agreement on how to make posters effective, a revolution was heralded in the designs of a small group of young, untutored California postermakers in the 1960s. Some of the most brilliant American posters have challenged the often-cited rule of poster graphics – that the text be legible. Wes Wilson, who gave form to the psychedelic-rock poster movement, reconfigured type to conform with abstract shapes and blocks of color. He developed what he called an easy-to-see but also mysterious form of lettering that immediately attracted attention.[7] These word-forms became a new visual language that served as a metaphor for an emerging freedom among youth who flocked to the San Francisco Bay Area in search of a developing music and the accompanying lifestyle. Wilson recalled:

> When I started doing posters, especially the posters in color . . . I think I selected my colors from my visual experience with LSD, along with what I'd learned as a printer. . . . Posters to me represented real departure points. I like the idea of filling up space, and I like to do my work freehand – no ruler and stuff.[8]

Yet his rock posters owed much to a European past. The style that Wilson made quintessentially American he acknowledged he had found in a catalogue for the November 1965 "Jugendstil and Expressionism" exhibit at the University of California at Berkeley, which included Vienna Secessionist lettering. Wilson said, "I was able to adapt it on almost all my posters from that point on."[9]

In their transition to promoting so-called psychedelic music, rock posters became American symbols, even as they continued to incorporate European elements. These posters were finally accepted and prized through the intervention of a masterful promoter, the European-born but later avidly American producer Bill Graham, who in the mid-1960s organized a series of now-legendary dance and rock-music concerts. He found the postermakers he encouraged and eventually made famous in Haight-

Ashbury, quite by accident. Though always working on tight schedules, Wes Wilson, Rick Griffin, Stanley Mouse, and Victor Moscoso managed to come up with original, striking, and intriguing images – from voluptuous women to cowboy paraphernalia – creating a visual vocabulary of unfailing inventiveness that made their increasingly sought-after posters uniquely effective.

In the mix of design and marketing, Graham remembers negotiating with his artists to get what he needed – information about the "when and where" of the events. Wilson and the other postermakers remember frustrating meetings with Graham where the battle lines between art and information were drawn. Graham would eventually get his way by shouting: "Don't get me to the point where you'll have total freedom, and then there'll be an asterisk somewhere pointing to the bottom, where there'll be an explanation of what's actually playing!"[10]

Though Bill Graham was sensitive to the power of Wes Wilson's work, he found it hard to keep his own opinions out of the discussions. As Graham said in an interview: "I'm not qualified; I'm not an artist, but I think there's always room for improvement. . . . There's room for the strengthening of a poster by means of better color combinations and more of a practical usage of words."[11] At the beginning Graham's authority had to be clearly established, and it took a long time to impress his position on the artists.

While many contributed to this genre's explosive use of color and typography, only Victor Moscoso brought to it the sophistication of his studio training at Yale, where he had studied with Josef Albers in his famous color course. In that milieu, students experimented to determine how hues and saturations would appear to change and flutter, to jump forward or pull back, depending on their juxtaposition. In his 1967 *Chambers Brothers* poster (plate 18), Moscoso handles this visual illusion with great skill.

More recently, the rock-poster sensibility that predominated through the 1970s has given way to a multitude of quite individual approaches. In the 1990s, many graphic devices are introduced to play on the tensions between high and low art. Art Chantry and others create exhibition and film posters that evoke the look of fliers advertising discount-store sales or spreads from Sears catalogues displaying tools (plate 30). There is American style in both the original use and in its amusing play with reinvention. The contrast bridges the gap between what the art crowd expects to see in a poster and what the mass "do it yourself" audience accepts.

Although often a powerful means of communication, posters acquire another life in the hands of collectors or in the more informal setting of a college dorm or teenager's room, where posters reflect personal identity. One critic adds that these almost private uses of a public medium often endorse controversial causes, such as draft resistance. In the privacy of the home, it is possible to align oneself with the postermaker who announces, *Girls Say Yes to Boys Who Say No* (plate 77), while one might be less willing to defend that position in public. The many celebrity posters now sold to mass markets depict personal fantasies through their use of such perennial favorites as Marilyn Monroe (plate 9), to such pinups of the day as the musical group Nine Inch Nails (plate 31).

OF RAISINS, CHICANOS, BREAD, AND JIM CROW

As they use either verbal or visual shorthand, postermakers may rely on stereotypes. Posters can use long-held assumptions about particular groups to paint with a broader brush across the social and cultural landscape. An unconscious aspect of the message embodied in many posters, such practices are now being challenged by minority groups. For example, an amusing vein of visual contrasts was created in the ad campaign for Levy's rye bread, ordinarily an "ethnic" Jewish product. The text, now famous, is "You Don't Have to Be Jewish to Love Levy's," while the picture is of a Native American (plate 54). More seriously, an ad for raisins is reconstructed as a poster to protest labor practices that affect a largely Chicano migrant workforce (plate 87).

In 1988 for the first time, the Bureau of the Census sought a more accurate way to count the Native American population, which until that time had been understandably suspicious of the United States's efforts to list or describe their tribes and their urban members. The new program was designed, with the advice of the Bureau of Indian Affairs, to reach out to the community without arousing their fears. Tom Oxendine, who was named leader of the effort, turned to the Santa Fe–based Institute of American Indian Arts, a Native American center for design and schooling in the arts. Posters were selected as a crucial medium. The school, Indian leaders, and the Census and Indian Affairs bureaus chose a Native American designer to produce five posters (plate 112). The messages for the set were "Name Your Tribe"; "Listen to the Drum"; and "Calling the Eagles." The series was used to encourage the cooperation that would eventually benefit the group, which received federal support based on the number of people counted. The posters did not explain the need for the count, but the design used familiar elements and was intended to allay fears that the census might be misused.

Jerry Ingram. *Listen to the Drum: Name Your Tribe. Answer the Census* (detail). See plate 112.

FIGHT! VOTE! WORK!

Most recent poster exhibitions have focused on the modernist styles of Bauhaus, Russian, and German posters, which are admired for their abstract design. By contrast, the strength and diversity of American posters have been shown in exhibitions devoted to specific events – the World War II poster show mounted at the National Archives, "Powers of Persuasion: Poster Art From World War II" (March 1994–February 1995); or "On the American Home Front" (Vanderbilt University Fine Arts Gallery, June–August 1994). But few surveys so far have aimed at highlighting the continuity of American contributions. In this volume, the emphasis is on series that have defined a visual approach, as did the circus and literary posters around the turn of the century, the United States government-sponsored posters for home-front propaganda during World Wars I and II and the Works Projects Administration (WPA), and the privately issued 1960s rock posters, as well as advertising and protest posters of the 1990s.

Propaganda posters have a long history. Widely dispersed in low-cost campaigns, they typically present a pointed, hard-hitting image that screams out its message. Among those issued during World War II, the award-winning *This Is the Enemy* (1942), by Victor Ancona and Karl Koehler (plate 67), represents a brilliant use of image and reflection. The American design vocabulary expanded rapidly with the influx of emigré artists, architects, and designers who left Europe at the outbreak of war for safety in the United States. Among these, Joseph Binder (plate 8), and Jean Carlu (plate 66), brought with them a modernist vision notable in the posters they completed in the late 1930s and 1940s.

The outrage that combines propaganda and protest is most memorably conveyed by the American Ben Shahn in *This Is Nazi Brutality* (1943). Here an ominous, hooded figure is confronted by a harrowing message of destruction which is plastered across the poster in a black-on-yellow Teletype then associated with disaster. An equally compelling use of symbols appears in Shahn's 1946 call for action. A pair of hands crumples the map of the United States, while the text urges "Break Reaction's Grip – Register – Vote" (plate 73). As modernist design was increasingly accepted in America, Shahn became the artist who best conveyed American challenges, among them the need to vote and to be aware of the character of presidential candidates (plate 72). Familiar phrases were employed to new advantage as American idioms, such as "Watch out for the man on the white horse." It is intriguing to speculate on how the then-head of the Office of War Information (OWI), the poet Archibald MacLeish, may have encouraged such creativity.

Most of these posters were home-front propaganda, and a significant number of them show imperiled children, muscular American men handling complex machinery, and strong women with their sleeves rolled up – competent women who can do the work required by hard times or war – who can maintain morale while the men do battle on far frontiers. The figures, design, and composition of these posters convey a sense of American power and purpose as well as a dedicated home front. Much of the propaganda effort had roots in the visuals of World War I; the famous *I Want You* of 1917 (plate 60) was recycled twenty-three years later for the new war.

One significant difference between the poster campaigns of the two wars was the way in which the United States government targeted the enemy. During World War I, the public reaction of German Americans to the vilifying, apelike caricature of the Hun clearly indicated that this approach was counterpersuasive, not believed, and therefore ineffective. Instead, MacLeish explained, "I hate Nazism and Fascism and all their words. But the campaigns of personal hatreds, of hatred for whole nations of human beings, are disgusting to me. There is a clear difference between the hatred of persons and the hatred of evil."[12] The OWI's posters usually succeeded in avoiding outright bigotry and instead celebrated a positive sense of American values. But other poster campaigns were hateful and demeaning, most notably the privately issued posters of the 1940s that bore scurrilous images of the Japanese people and gained wide circulation during the war in the Pacific.

In the ambitious poster program directed to the home front, there were also miscalculations and missed opportunities, one of which has become legend in its now obvious lack of judgment. Following President Franklin D. Roosevelt's famous 1941 speech in which he named and described the four freedoms – of the press and religion, and from fear and want – the well-known illustrator Norman Rockwell offered to paint images illustrating these concepts and then adapt them for posters. Initially his offer was turned down, possibly because many OWI designers were not illustrators, as had been the case in the government's war poster campaign of 1915, but artists aligned with fine art traditions.[13] Not surprisingly, the *Saturday Evening Post,* which had commissioned much of Rockwell's previous work, had him do these paintings which first appeared on successive covers in 1943; their effectiveness was instantly evident.[14]

In that same year, Rockwell's *Four Freedoms* were issued as posters, each in several sizes. One such edition became the very successful incentive given to purchasers of war bonds. Possibly no set of posters has been reproduced in such great quantity or more widely collected – even today the set is valued highly. The prepara-

tory study for the first in the series, *Save Freedom of Speech,* an oil and pencil on board given to a Curtis Publishing employee, went to auction in 1997. The sale of this previously unknown sketch excited wide interest and a high price.

If the immediate popularity of Norman Rockwell's scenes of small-town neighbors acting out the Four Freedoms in intimate American views came as a surprise to the government officials who approved poster designs, the need to use posters was never in question. What had changed was the direction of the postermaking process. In 1917, soon after the United States entered World War I, the Society of Illustrators met to offer its help in the war effort. Its president, Charles Dana Gibson, had received a telegram requesting help from George Creel, the director of the Committee on Public Information. Soon after, the Division of Pictorial Publicity was created. A way to reach the public, including those who might otherwise not attend meetings or watch propaganda movies, was required:

> *The billboard was something that caught even the most indifferent eye. . . . What we wanted – what we had to have – were posters that represented the best work of the best artists – posters into which the masters of the pen and brush poured heart and soul as well as genius. Looking the field over, we decided upon Charles Dana Gibson as the man best suited to lead the army of artists.*[15]

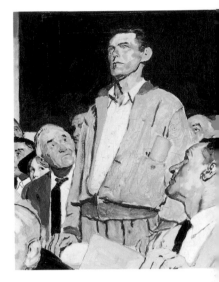

Norman Rockwell. Oil sketch for *Save Freedom of Speech.* 1943. Oil and pencil on board, 20 x 16 in. (50.8 x 41.9 cm). Vivian and Stanley Picheny.

Norman Rockwell. *Save Freedom of Speech* (detail). See plate 96.

In all, the Pictorial Division proposed 700 designs to fifty-eight separate government agencies and patriotic committees and thus made their influence felt in the broader war effort. The artists usually donated their work – a noteworthy and altruistic act, since many of them could market sketches for prices ranging from $1,000 to $10,000. With this innovative first-time use of artists to make war posters, the War Department recognized the value of art to form public opinion – what we recognize today as an aspect of propaganda.

Other government initiatives also took form and reached the public through posters. The Works Projects Administration offered advice on safety, health, and other topics of general interest, often employing artists who had immigrated to the United States in the mid-1930s. By World War II, more than 5,000 posters had been issued, and many more were submitted for consideration. Some of these pencil sketches still exist and are kept in the National Archives.

METHODS AND TECHNIQUES

Nowhere is the mix of commerce, design, and art more evident in posters than in their actual production. Between 1895 and 1995, many printing techniques were available and used concurrently. The traditional woodblock required the maker to draw the design on the block in reverse, cutting away the nonprinting background and thus leaving only the design elements to be inked and printed. This method was used by Edward Penfield, and from time to time by others who wanted to achieve a rough, handcrafted look.

Lithography, widely used in commercial printing, employed scarce and heavy limestone blocks. These blocks allowed autographic drawing and gave the poster-maker freedom to design, create with many colors, and continue to make changes in the course of successive impressions. Over time, lithographers have used a variety of surfaces, including aluminum, resin, and gels.

Probably the most significant advance in printing prior to the advent of computer technology was offset printing, in which the ink is transferred from the plate to the paper via rollers. In both letterpress and woodblock, the raised areas receive the ink, and thus print. In the process known generically as offset lithography, the plate can be produced in many ways, but it is neither cut away nor raised.

The many variants of offset printing differ in detail and application, and their names often do not clearly describe details of each particular technique. Once the most common method of reproducing posters, lithographic reproduction produces a continuous ink tone, which is a marker for much of the medium. Many offset printing systems employ photographic materials that are translated into screen prints; their characteristic tiny dot patterns are best visible when magnified. To achieve color in offset printing, photographic separations are employed. Each separation, made as a plate that carries ink, superimposes an additional hue, thus altering the hues left by previous impressions on the printed image. Accurate registration (or alignment) of the series of separated images is crucial to obtaining a good reproduction. Fidelity of color, or obtaining the desired hue in an abstract design, is ultimately controlled by the dispersion of ink via the dot screens on each successive plate.

The dot screen has become a Pop art symbol. Artists such as Roy Lichtenstein have employed the type of imagery seen in comic books and newspaper comics – for all the decades of this century, the humblest and most democratic of printed icons – but painted them "by hand" at an enormously enlarged scale. The artist adapts image style and dot screen to a wry, irreverent format with the cachet of "fine art."

Edward Penfield, Waltham Manufacturing Co. *Orient Cycles* (detail). See plate 44.

Few of the many terms identifying the reproduction media of posters are easily understood. Each collection favors its own vocabulary for indicating the processes, using qualifications such as "photo," "mechanical," even "commercial," and "color." The phrase "photomechanical lithograph" covers a variety of methods of offset reproduction and is often used by collectors when they are unsure how a specific poster was printed.

In addition, many forms of printing coexist. Some of the most effective posters are issued by artist's collectives like the Royal Chicano Air Force (RCAF),[16] which pragmatically seek out the most economical and quickest printing and distribution methods. Wes Wilson points out the contrast between the relatively labor-intensive West Coast rock posters and the later high-speed press runs of huge numbers of posters by commercially knowledgeable artists like Peter Max.[17]

MODERN AMERICAN STYLE

Like many nineteenth-century photographs, posters were issued by studios and companies for whom the postermaker often worked anonymously. This was true for the Cincinnati-based Strobridge Lithography Co., an active posterworks.[18] Strobridge was a sort of cradle for many of the more distinguished younger Americans, who received their first training there as journeyman lithographers. It is not easy to trace their individual designs, for names never appear upon the gorgeous or gaudy Barnum and Forepaugh posters in which, for a period, Americans found most of their art.

Early Penfield and Bradley posters were produced by color lithography, but eventually this method was phased out because it was too cumbersome and labor-intensive and, in the hands of some, rougher in its linear silhouette. But the use of photography and offset became available to postermakers in the 1920s, making larger runs possible, lowering costs, and speeding the whole production process. In recent years, the computer and desktop publishing have again transformed poster-making. As each new software program permits more choices, posters surprise us with their expanding possibilities.

In the 1990s, a series of ever-changing technologies encourage creative, individual solutions to problems of communication. This technology affects the role of posters in art, public relations, advertising, and community group advocacy. Since the 1950s, supplanted by television as a means of reaching out to large groups, posters have increasingly been targeted to specific facets of a population – according to ethnicity or age, for example. Museums have increasingly produced posters to promote and commemorate special exhibitions, and it is now possible to announce and advertise with ever greater facility these exhibitions by means of ever simpler digital production systems.

New ways to create posters, together with the intensive use of advertising, combine to suggest that posters in the 1990s and beyond will be produced at an increasing rate. What makes the present survey of American posters both compelling and memorable to the larger public is the range and originality of many poster series. But graphically striking as they are, it is their content – the reminders of past events, film stars, the need to fight wars – that captures our attention.

How were these posters seen in their original contexts? American posters are encountered most often as a kind of "wallpaper" in shopping malls or on our streets – though many government posters that advise Americans on various issues are often placed in offices or small work areas. The size of the available space and the competition for it often control the look and size of posters. Today, posters are frequently seen as the startlingly bright stock of museum shops, at travel agency desks, and in college dorms. Major poster auctions in New York and San Francisco offer collectors opportunities to buy from a stock usually arranged by theme – circus, film, performance, country of origin, and so forth.

In this country, the audience for posters used to be very broad, patriotic, and for the most part, English-speaking. Many community groups now address their audiences in other languages, and with symbols that have particular cultural meanings. Some poster artists use all-purpose icons to convey a message (e.g., Lichtenstein, plate 103, and Rand, plate 7). Details of commonplace services, such as David Goines's poster for Chez Panisse (plate 57), tell their story to everyone – language is unimportant. But this approach no longer engages the American political audience, which could be addressed in a single voice from World War I through the end of World War II. Today, citizens are not engaged in the political process; they do not vote in large numbers, they have turned from public meetings, and they have lost their trust in government. To address a large number of disparate groups, today's postermakers narrow their scope and aim a particular message at a specific group. The postermaker can rely on such tightly focused groups – museum visitors, opera lovers, working women – to share a specialized vocabulary and frame of reference.

Perhaps the most fascinating aspect of American posters is their genius for mirroring and enlarging American cultural issues. They mix art and commerce; they picture many forms of advocacy. Although we recognize that our response to many

Overleaf: Peter Gee. *Martin Luther King, Jr.* (detail). See plate 76.

early American posters involves nostalgia for the times and events of our history, the most significant thread in our response to posters of all periods is a willingness to accept the disappearance of the distinction between high and low art. This is American style.

NOTES

1. Susan Sontag. "Posters: Advertisement, art, political artifact, commodity," in Donald Stermer, ed., *The Art of Revolution: 96 Posters from Castro's Cuba, 1959–1970* (New York: McGraw Hill, 1970).

2. Katherine McCoy, as quoted by Elena G. Millie in "College Poster Art," *Art Journal* 44 (spring 1984): 60.

3. John Merten, "Stone by Stone along a Hundred Years with the House of Strobridge," *Bulletin of the Historical and Philosophical Society of Ohio* 8, no. 1 (Jan. 1950): 15–22.

4. See Walton Rawls, *Wake Up, America! World War I and the American Poster* (New York: Abbeville Press, Inc., 1979): 81. The quote is taken from a long, informative analysis of the beginnings of World War I and its posters considered in their historical context with anecdotes, news reports, and letters.

5. David W. Kiehl, *American Art Posters of the 1890s in The Metropolitan Museum of Art, Including the Leonard A. Lauder Collection* (New York: Metropolitan Museum of Art, 1987): 13.

6. See Roberta Waddell Wong, *American Posters of the Nineties* (Boston: Boston Public Library, 1974).

7. As described by Walter Medeiros in *San Francisco Rock Poster Art* (San Francisco: San Francisco Museum of Modern Art, 1976): 5–7.

8. Paul D. Grushkin, *The Art of Rock* (New York: Abbeville Press, Inc., 1987): 72.

9. Ibid.

10. Grushkin, 73.

11. Notes from a personal interview the author conducted in 1968 with Graham around the corner from the Fillmore Auditorium in San Francisco.

12. As quoted by Stacey Bredhoff in *Powers of Persuasion: Poster Art from World War II* (Washington, D.C.: National Archives Office of Public Programs, 1994): 28.

13. Rawls, 149.

14. For a fascinating account of these events see Stuart Murray and James McCabe, *Norman Rockwell's Four Freedoms: Images that Inspire a Nation* (Stockbridge, Mass.: Berkshire House Publishers, 1993).

15. Rawls, 149–50.

16. Previously known as the Rebel Chicano Air Force, the group's name is a send-up of the acronym used for the Royal Canadian Air Force.

17. Grushkin, 88.

18. Joseph Pennell, as quoted in Merten, 2.

Guide to Postermaking Terms

As posters have been printed in many ways throughout the one hundred years of this survey, the list outlined below was developed to describe the various technologies. If the lending institution or collector specified a term, that term is used. If no medium was noted, the medium has been determined using the most general terminology, as most modern posters include a complex mix of printing processes that cannot be identified by mere examination. The new digital processes add to the choices available in offset photomechanical printing. Though woodblock, stone lithography, and silkscreen are used less frequently in large poster editions, they are still occasionally in use today.

WOODBLOCK printing involves carving a relief image in reverse on a block of wood. Ink is then applied to the carving, and the image is transferred from the inked block to the paper.

LETTERPRESS TYPE is another form of printing in which a relief image is inked and printed directly onto paper.

LITHOGRAPHY is based on the principle that oil and water do not mix. Using oil-based ink or a grease crayon, an image is drawn on a flat stone or metal plate. Next, water is applied to the surface and is repelled by the areas where oil-based images have been drawn. The entire surface is then coated with an oil-based ink that adheres only to the areas drawn in oil ink or crayon. The image is then printed on paper. The popularity of this process grew because thousands of exact replicas could be made, which were like drawings on paper, without degradation of the image.

COLOR LITHOGRAPHY is essentially the same process as basic lithography. In this process, however, each color is printed separately with careful alignment or registration.

OFFSET LITHOGRAPHY, another form of the lithographic process, transfers the image to paper from a "positive" drawing (rather than from reverse or relief images used in other methods). A large rubber roller picks up the image from the plate and then rolls it onto the paper surface. Thus, the paper never actually touches the original plate image. Offset lithography replaced direct lithography once the technology was perfected. It made possible much larger print runs of commercial images such as posters.

PHOTO-OFFSET, or photomechanical offset, is based on the earlier process of photolithography. A photograph of the original image is passed through a half-tone screen to render it into a pattern of dots, and it is then converted chemically into a lithographic image. The dotted image is finally printed mechanically on paper using an offset press.

SILKSCREENING, which was introduced around 1907, presses ink through a fine screen onto paper. A stencil of an image is placed on a taut screen with paper underneath. Ink is then spread on top and forced through the screen onto the paper with a squeegee. Unlike photo-offset, silkscreening allows the artist to vary the colors and patterns while printing.

SERIGRAPHY is the term many artists prefer to describe screenprinting.

DIGITAL PRINTMAKING, which has been used since the early 1990s, utilizes digital computer technology and design tools such as image scanners, design software, and image editing programs. Computer-generated images can be reproduced using either traditional printing methods or digital printing technology. This process offers almost unlimited possibilities as a postermaking medium for the twenty-first century.

AMERICAN EVENTS

1. UNKNOWN

Strobridge Lithographing Company. *The Barnum & Bailey Greatest Show on Earth: Ski Sailing.* 1907. Color lithograph, 28¾ x 38¹¹⁄₁₆ in. (73 x 98 cm). Cincinnati Art Museum, gift of the Strobridge Lithographing Company Library.

2. UNKNOWN

Strobridge Lithographing Company. *The Barnum & Bailey Greatest Show on Earth: Mooney's "Giants."* 1913. Color lithograph, 28⅛ x 38¾ in. (72.8 x 98.3 cm). Cincinnati Art Museum, gift of the Strobridge Lithographing Company Library.

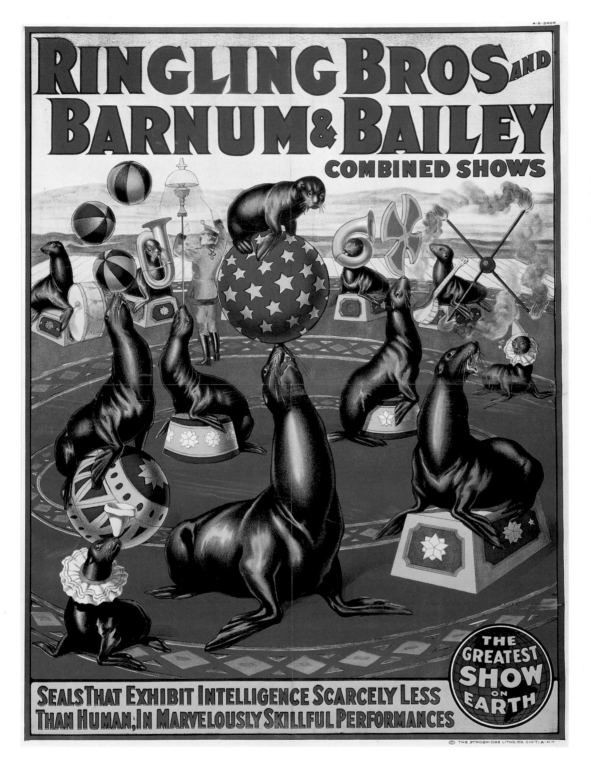

4. UNKNOWN

Strobridge Lithographing
Company. *Charles Frohman
Presents Peter Pan.* 1907. Two
color lithographs on page,
30⅛ x 40¼ in. (76.6 x 102.2 cm).
Cincinnati Art Museum, gift of
the Strobridge Lithographing
Company Library.

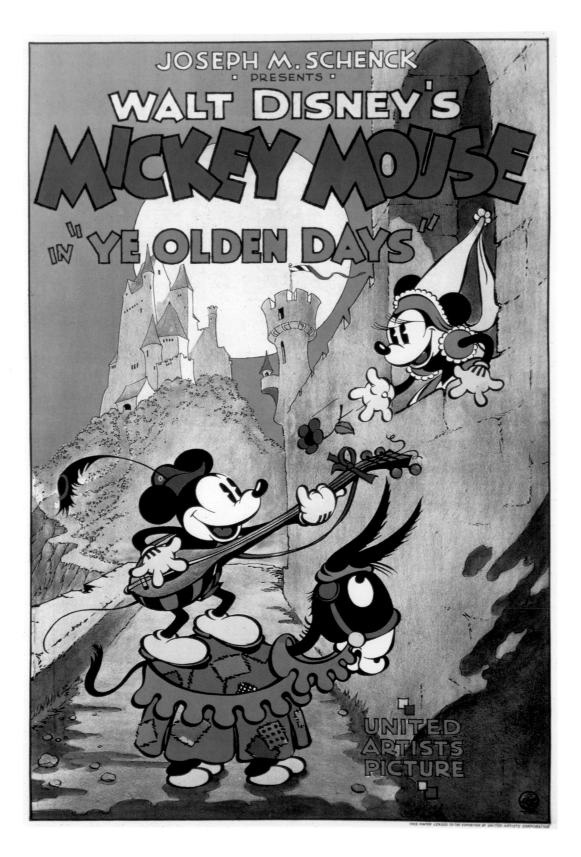

6. CARKEN

Federal Art Project (Chicago). *Brookfield Zoo.* 1936. Color silkscreen, 14 x 22 in. (35.6 x 56 cm). Library of Congress, Prints and Photographs Division.

Among the most effective graphics ever produced for this zoo, the strong outline of this crouched animal was drawn by Carken, a postermaker working in the Chicago office of the Federal Art Project. Although little is known about the maker, this poster's technical brilliance and effective communication are typical of the art produced in this workshop.

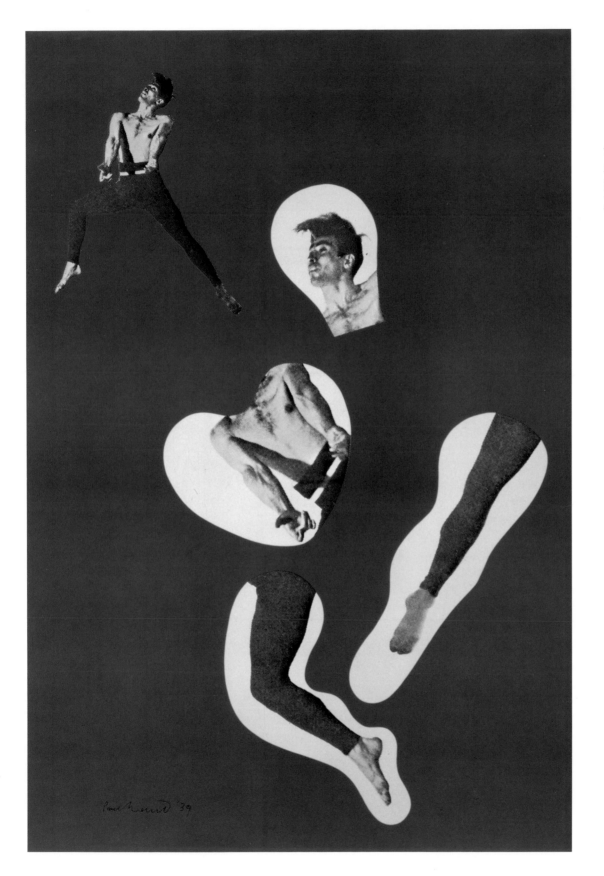

10. SAUL BASS

Vertigo. 1958. Lithograph,
10⅔ x 41 in. (27 x 104.1 cm).
Pacific Film Archives, University
Art Museum, University of
California at Berkeley.

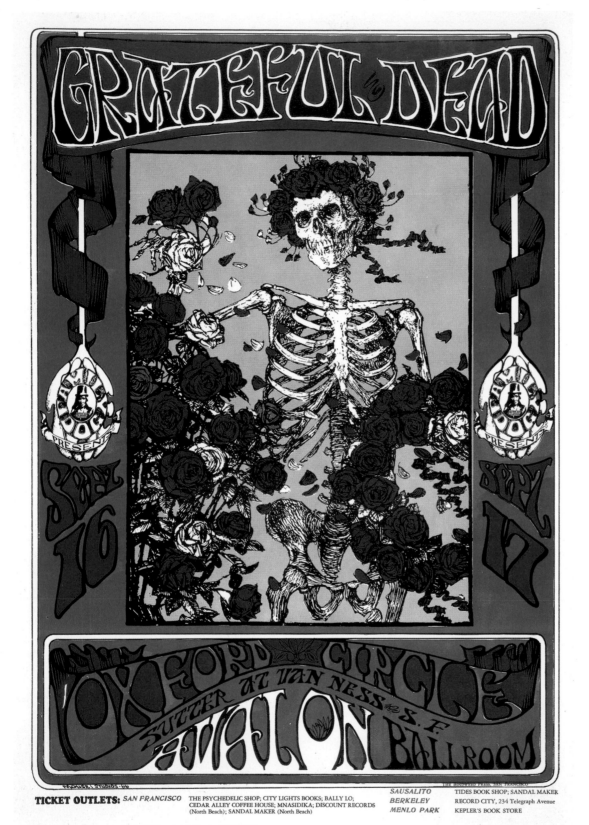

11. STANLEY MOUSE

Grateful Dead, Oxford Circle (Avalon Ballroom). 1966. Offset lithograph, 20 x 14¼ in. (50.8 x 30.2 cm). The Oakland Museum of California, gift of Family Dog Productions.

12. WES WILSON

West Coast Lithograph Co. (San Francisco). *Bill Graham Presents . . . Captain Beefhart & His Magic Band, Chocolate Watch Band, Fillmore Auditorium.* 1966. Color lithograph, 19 x 13 ¾ in. (48.3 x 34.9 cm). Mr. and Mrs. W. Robert Johnston.

13. WES WILSON

Bill Graham Presents.
Presented in Dance-Concert by Bill Graham: Jefferson Airplane.
1966. Color lithograph,
22 x 14 in. (55.9 x 35.6 cm).
Mr. and Mrs. W. Robert Johnston.

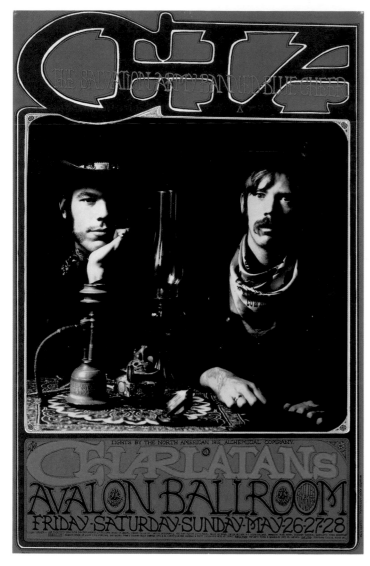

14. RICK GRIFFIN

Family Dog Publishing.
*Charlatans: The Salvation
Army Banned Blue Cheer.* 1967.
Color lithograph, 22 x 14 in.
(55.9 x 35.6 cm). Mr. and Mrs.
W. Robert Johnston.

15. RICK GRIFFIN

*Charlatans: The 13th Floor
Elevators.* 1967. Color lithograph,
22 x 14 in. (55.9 x 35.6 cm).
Leslie, Judy, and Gabri Schreyer,
and Alice Schreyer Batko.

16. BOB FRIED

Charlatans: The Youngbloods and the Other Half. 1967. Color lithograph, 22 x 14 in. (55.9 x 35.6 cm). Leslie, Judy, and Gabri Schreyer, and Alice Schreyer Batko.

Apparently it was seeing rock posters by Stanley Mouse and Alton Kelley that prompted Rick Griffin to move from Los Angeles to the San Francisco Bay Area where he began designing posters to advertise the Charlatans' rock concerts. In this three-part series, Griffin's favorite motifs, mainly stemming from the "Wild West" – brimmed hats, gas lighting, and prospector style – are prominent. In the third poster, Fried continues the style and symbols that Griffin established for the Charlatans.

17. VICTOR MOSCOSO

Neon Rose. *Big Brother and the Holding Company.* 1967. Color lithograph, 20 x 13¾ in. (50.8 x 34.9 cm). Mr. and Mrs. W. Robert Johnston.

18. VICTOR MOSCOSO

Neon Rose. *The Chambers Brothers.* 1967. Color lithograph, 20 x 13¾ in. (50.8 x 34.9 cm). Leslie, Judy, and Gabri Schreyer, and Alice Schreyer Batko.

20. VICTOR MOSCOSO AND RICK GRIFFIN

Bill Graham Presents in San Francisco: Jimi Hendrix Experience. 1968. Color lithograph, 21½ x 14⅛ in. (54.6 x 34.9 cm). Mr. and Mrs. W. Robert Johnston.

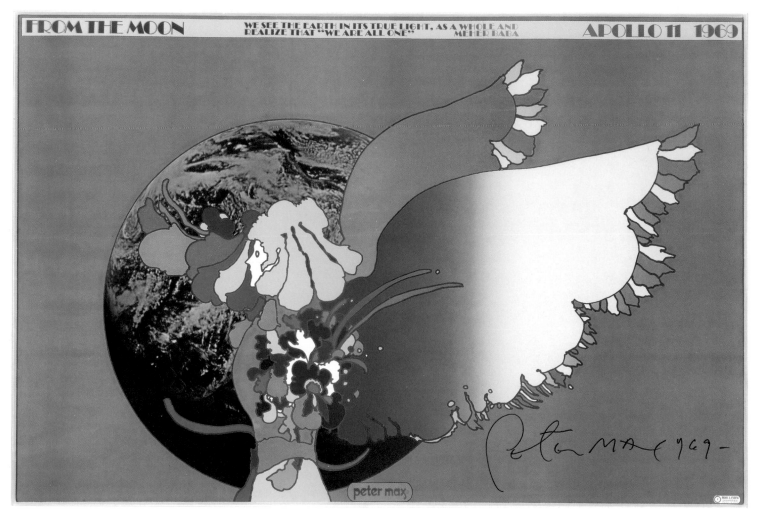

21. PETER MAX

From the Moon. 1969. Mechanical reproduction, 24 x 36 in. (61 x 91.4 cm). Penny and Moreton Binn, New York.

Peter Max brings an exotic mixture of influences to his graphic design, from his childhood in China to his sense of the psychedelic.

For *From the Moon,* diverse factors play into the celebration of this "other wordly" event – the race to the moon by two world powers, the United States of America and the Soviet Union, won in dramatic fashion by the United States in 1969.

23. RUPERT GARCIA

Inaugural Exhibit of Mexican and Chicano Art. 1975. Serigraph, 22⅝ x 16½ in. (57.1 x 41.9 cm). National Museum of American Art, Smithsonian Institution, gift of Tomás Ybarra-Frausto.

24. PAUL DAVIS

For Colored Girls. 1976.
Lithograph, 81 x 41 in.
(205.7 x 104.1 cm).
PosterAmerica.

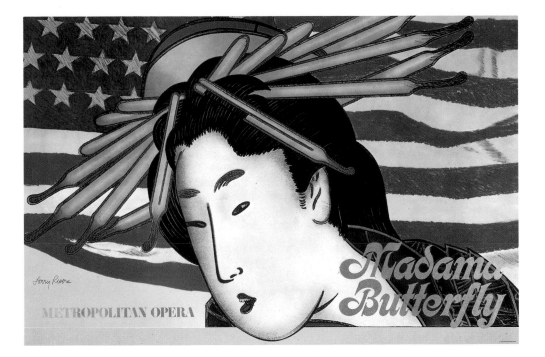

25. LARRY RIVERS

Circle Gallery (New York). *Madama Butterfly – Metropolitan Opera.* 1978. Offset lithograph, 24 x 35⅘ in. (61 x 91 cm). Library of Congress, Prints and Photographs Division. © 1998 Larry Rivers/Licensed by VAGA, New York, N.Y.

26. PATRICK NAGEL

Mirage Editions (Santa Monica, California). *The Paper Mill, Los Angeles.* 1980. Color silkscreen, 25⅖ x 17 in. (64 x 43 cm). Library of Congress, Prints and Photographs Division.

27. ROBERT RAUSCHENBERG

Lincoln Center Film Society
(New York). *20th New York Film
Festival.* 1982. Offset lithograph,
45 ¼ x 30 ⅓ in. (115 x 77 cm).
Library of Congress, Prints and
Photographs Division. © 1998
Robert Rauschenberg/Licensed
by VAGA, New York, N.Y.

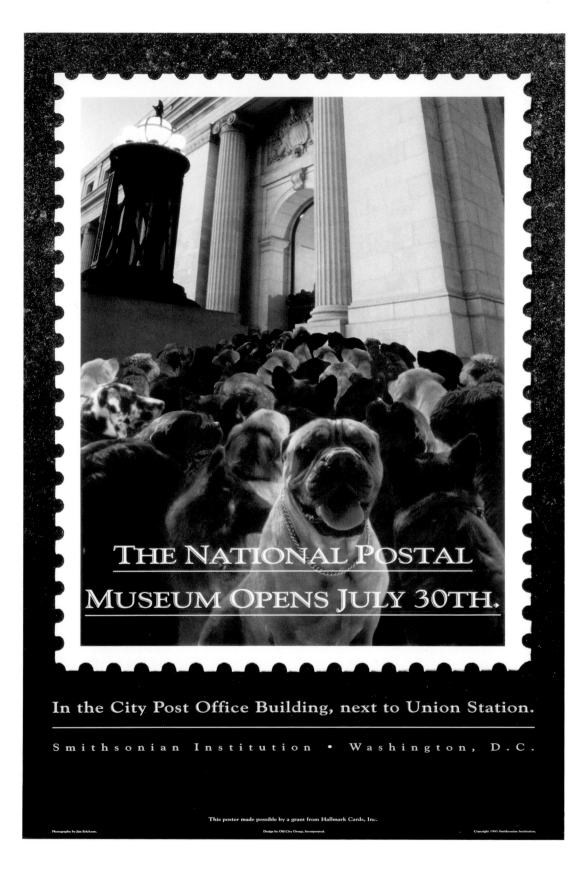

THE NATIONAL POSTAL MUSEUM OPENS JULY 30TH.

In the City Post Office Building, next to Union Station.

Smithsonian Institution • Washington, D.C.

This poster made possible by a grant from Hallmark Cards, Inc.

Photography by Jim Erickson.   Design by Old City Group, Incorporated.   Copyright 1993 Smithsonian Institution.

28. OLD CITY GROUP (DESIGNER) AND JIM ERICKSON (PHOTOGRAPHER)

National Postal Museum, Smithsonian Institution. *The National Postal Museum Opens July 30th.* 1993. Offset lithograph, 36 x 24 in. (91.5 x 61 cm). National Museum of American Art, Smithsonian Institution.

Photographer Jim Erickson received howling support from dog owners in Raleigh, North Carolina, when he put out the call for models for this project. Created to announce the opening of the Smithsonian's National Postal Museum, the ad agency was well aware of the potential for public apathy at the notion of a monument to letter carriers. This tongue-in-cheek image represents an early application of what was, in 1993, cutting-edge digital technology, seamlessly merging over fifty photographs of individual dogs and distinct backgrounds into a composite whole.

29. DAVID LANCE GOINES

Berkeley Conference Center & Visitors Bureau (Howl). 1993. Photo-offset lithograph, 24 x 17⅜ in. (61 x 44.1 cm). Private collection.

Goines's personal experiences as a student at Berkeley provide a subtext for this work. When he first read Alan Ginsberg's poem "Howl," it was illegal to send it through the mail. "We read it clandestinely in our English class, and now in this poster another generation was being introduced to the poem without knowing that a lot of people had fought hard to preserve the First Amendment rights involved. . . ."

30. ART CHANTRY

Kustom Kulture. 1994.
Serigraph, 33 ½ x 22 ⅜ in.
(85.7 x 56.8 cm). National
Museum of American Art,
Smithsonian Institution, gift
of the artist.

Like many of the poster
designers in this exhibition,
Chantry has been recog-
nized for his brash, hard-
edged approach – applied
in his case to Seattle rock
music groups. "I began,"
he said, "because the punk
style was like what I was
doing in my own way."
He considers himself a
"folk artist for a merchant/
technical culture."

2

DESIGN TO SELL

32. WILLIAM H. BRADLEY

Stone & Kimball (Chicago). *The Chap-Book: Thanksgiving Number*. 1895. Color lithograph, 19 5/8 x 18 7/8 in. (49.9 x 33.8 cm). The Baltimore Museum of Art, gift of Alfred and Dana Himmelrich, Baltimore.

Through his posters and book covers, Will Bradley is credited with introducing the American public to the undulating curves of the Art Nouveau style. This holiday announcement for the literary periodical *The Chap-Book* was so enthusiastically collected that it was reportedly out of print in less than two months.

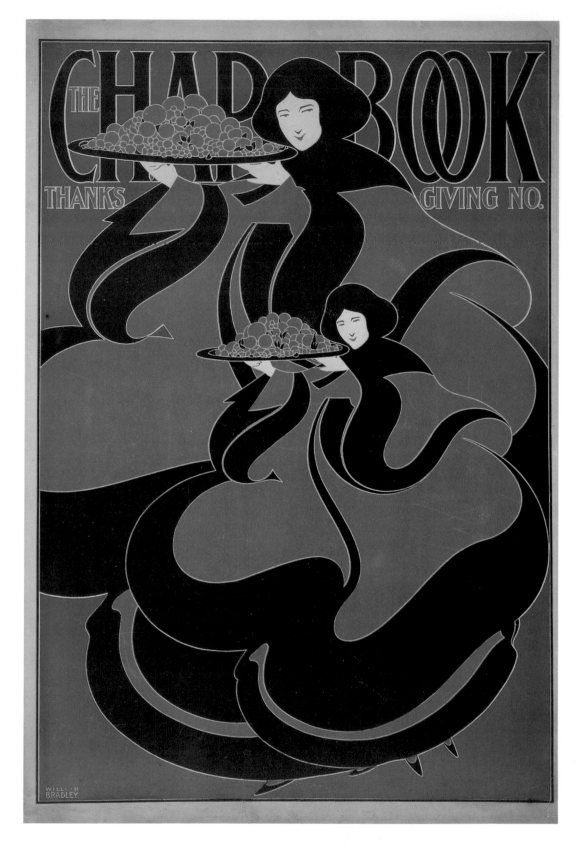

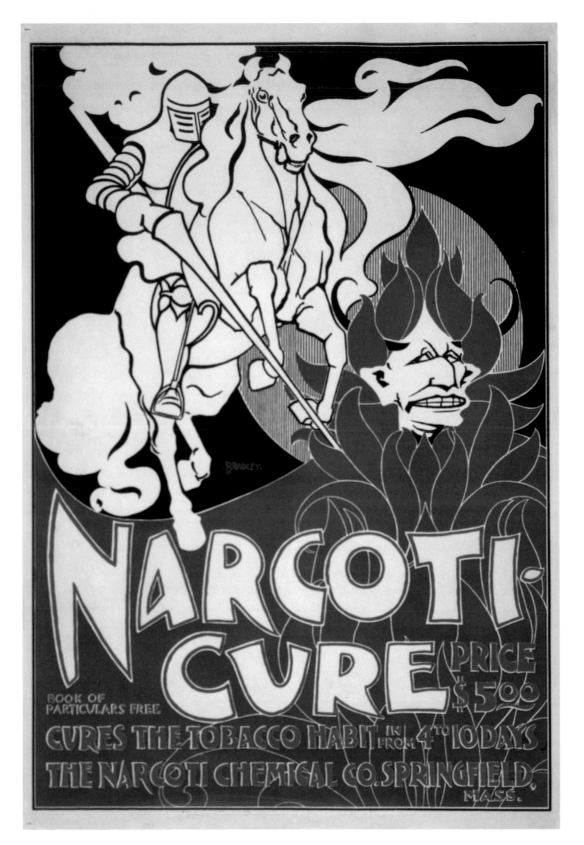

33. WILLIAM H. BRADLEY

Narcoti Chemical Co. (Springfield, Mass.). *Narcoti-Cure*. 1895. Color lithograph, 20 x 13 ½ in. (50 x 34 cm). The Baltimore Museum of Art, gift of Alfred and Dana Himmelrich, Baltimore.

Will Bradley's advertisement for the Narcoti Chemical Company of Springfield, Massachusetts, was produced shortly after he moved to that city around 1895. In the 1890s few scientific studies linked cigarette smoking to disease. Opposition to tobacco was often based on the belief that its use weakened moral character, a view promoted with evangelical zeal by activist Lucy Page Gaston, who founded the Anti-Cigarette League in 1899. Thus Bradley's symbolic characterization of tobacco as a demon was commonly appreciated, though the curative value of using a "narcotic" to treat tobacco addiction remains suspect.

34. MAYNARD DIXON

Overland. 1895. Lithograph, 18⅛ x 12¾ in. (45.9 x 32.4 cm). Delaware Art Museum, gift of Mrs. John Sloan.

Although Maynard Dixon was known as an artist of the West, similar in stature to Russell and Remington, he made his living by illustrating books, designing posters and covers for magazines, and painting murals and billboards. Independent of the changing aesthetics in the mainstream of the American art world, his style remained vividly realistic.

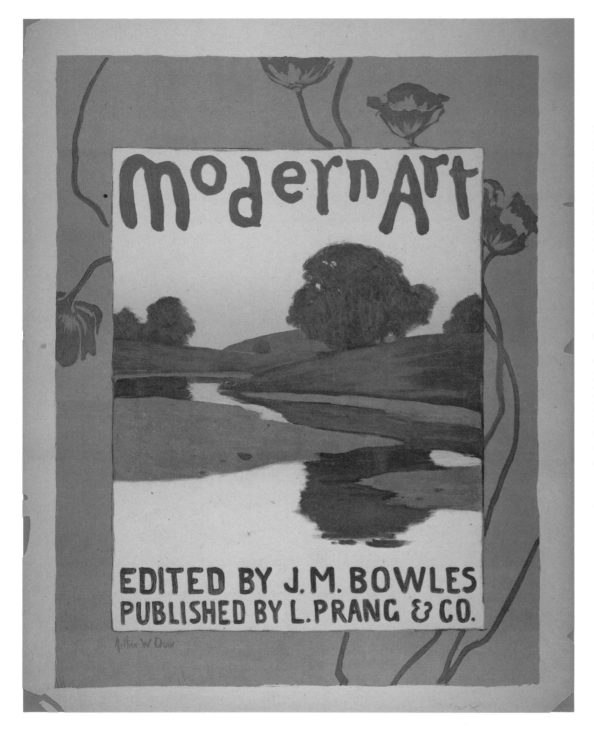

35. ARTHUR WESLEY DOW

Louis Prang & Co. (Boston). *Modern Art.* 1895. Color lithograph, 20 x 15 ¾ in. (50.8 x 40 cm). National Museum of American Art, Smithonian Institution, gift of Gary and Brenda and Harrison Ruttenberg.

The nearly abstract composition and geometric placement of this landscape in a floral frame demonstrate the strong influence of Japanese design on Arthur Wesley Dow's work. Reproduced from a woodcut by printer and *Modern Art* publisher Louis Prang, the poster was available as a free benefit to the journal's subscribers and to the general public for twenty-five cents in stamps.

36. FLORENCE LUNDBORG

William Doxey (San Francisco).
The Lark (November, 1895).
1895. Color woodblock,
16⅜ x 9⅞ in. (41.6 x 18.9 cm).
The Oakland Museum of
California, gift of Museum
Donors Acquisition Fund.

37. LOUIS JOHN RHEAD

The *New York Sun. Read The
Sun.* 1895. Color lithograph,
46¹³⁄₁₆ x 29 in. (118.9 x 73.7 cm).
The Metropolitan Museum of
Art, Leonard A. Lauder
Collection of American Posters,
gift of Leonard A. Lauder, 1984.

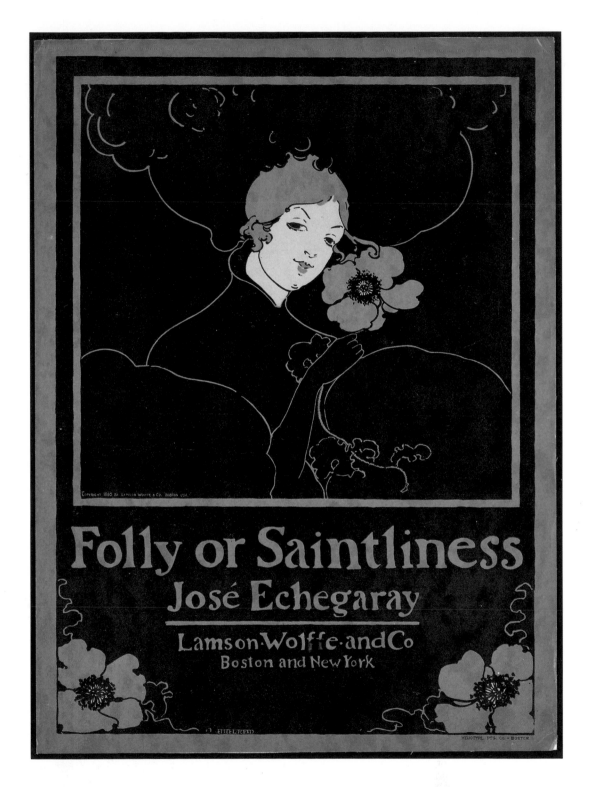

Folly or Saintliness
José Echegaray

Lamson·Wolffe·and Co
Boston and New York

38. ETHEL REED

Lamson, Wolffe & Co. (Boston), printed by Heliotype Printing Co. (Boston). *Folly or Saintliness.* 1895. Heliotype, 20¼ x 14⅞ in. (51.4 x 37.8 cm). National Museum of American Art, Smithsonian Institution, gift of Ms. S. Lavine.

Ethel Reed was one of a distinguished few among female illustrators working in the 1890s who gained recognition during their lifetimes. Best known for her posters advertising romantic novels with fresh-faced young girls surrounded by symbolic floral designs, Reed also illustrated the books and designed the covers and endpapers as well.

40. JOHN HENRY TWACHTMAN

Stone & Kimball (New York). *The Damnation of Theron Ware (or Illumination).* 1896. Color lithograph, 21 x 13 in. (53.3 x 33 cm). National Museum of American Art, Smithsonian Institution, museum purchase.

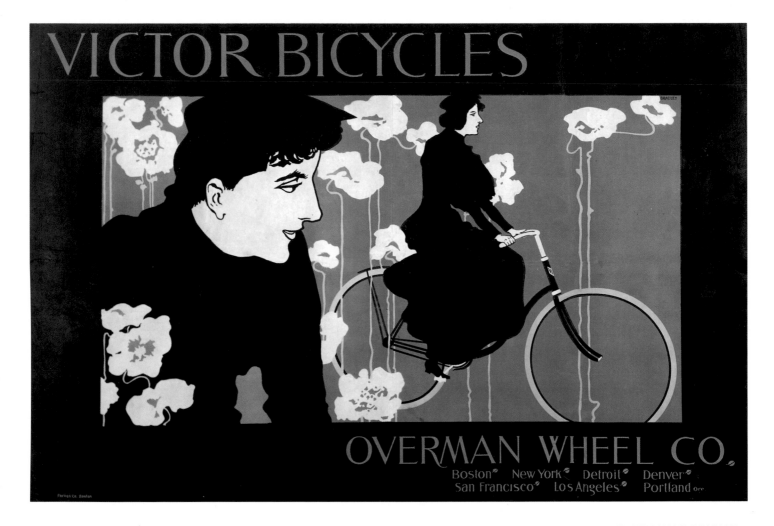

41. WILLIAM H. BRADLEY

The Overman Wheel Co.
(Chicopee Falls, Mass.). *Victor
Bicycles.* 1896. Color lithograph,
27 x 40¾ in. (68.6 x 103.5 cm).
The Baltimore Museum of
Art, gift of Alfred and Dana
Himmelrich, Baltimore.

42. EDWARD PENFIELD

Harper & Brothers
(New York). *Harper's June.*
1896. Color lithograph,
18¾ x 13⅞ in. (47.6 x 35.2 cm).
Virginia Museum of Fine Arts.

Edward Penfield noted,
"A poster has to play to
the public over the variety
stage . . . to come on with
a personality of its own
and to remain but a few
moments. We are a little
tired of the very serious
nowadays, and a little friv-
olity is refreshing."

A rising literacy rate in
the nineteenth century contributed to a growing number of literary periodicals
and trade journals. Edward
Penfield's spare, expressive
designs for *Harper's* magazine were meant to appeal
to, and often featured,
stylish men and women of
the middle or upper classes.
Influenced by outstanding
French postermakers such
as Jules Chéret and Henri
de Toulouse-Lautrec,
Penfield's posters have also
been described as narra-
tives or vignettes that
reveal a uniquely American
character.

43. EDWARD PENFIELD

Stearns Manufacturing Company. *Ride a Stearns and Be Content.* 1896. Color lithograph, 54⅝ x 40 in. (138.7 x 101.6 cm). The Metropolitan Museum of Art, Leonard A. Lauder Collection of American Posters, gift of Leonard A. Lauder, 1984.

The pursuit of physical and mental health through outdoor recreation made cycling a popular Victorian sport. This sophisticated Penfield image of a fashionable, "independent" female accurately reveals changing societal expectations about the roles of women.

44. EDWARD PENFIELD

Waltham Manufacturing Co. (New York). *Orient Cycles.* c. 1896. Color lithograph, 41½ x 27½ in. (105.4 x 69.9 cm). Collection Merrill C. Berman.

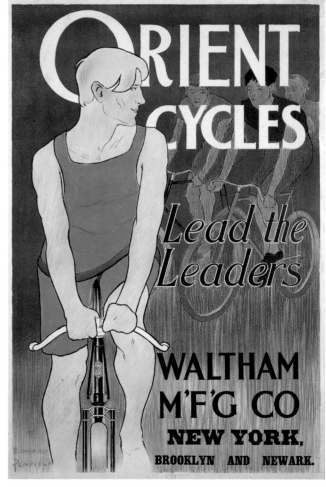

45. JOHN SLOAN

Copeland and Day (Boston). *Cinder-Path Tales.* 1896. Color lithograph, 23 ⅝ x 13 ⅝ in. (60 x 34.6 cm). Brenda and Gary Ruttenberg.

Sloan said that his posters were done from "memory and imagination of real life. . . . Of the French poster artists I was most influenced by Steinlen. I liked the humanism with which he drew people, and learned from him technical devices about using crayon to make shading that could be used for linecut reproduction. It was mostly from a study of Japanese prints that I found fresh ideas about design discovered in observing everyday life."

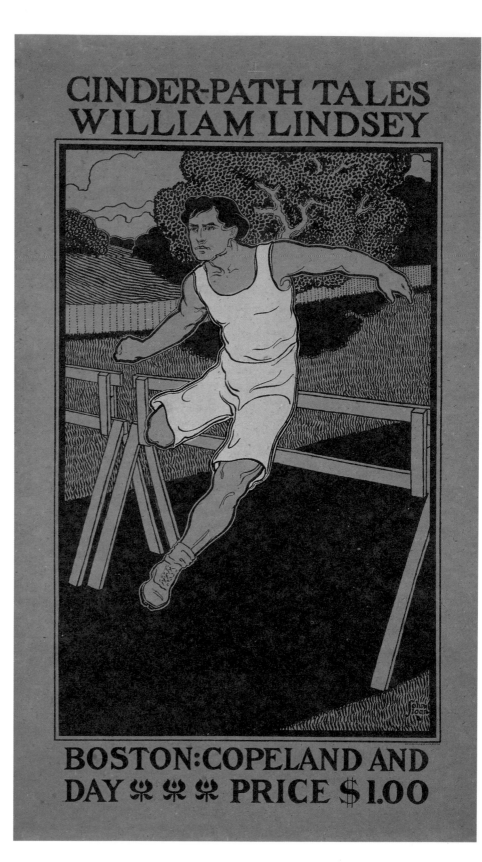

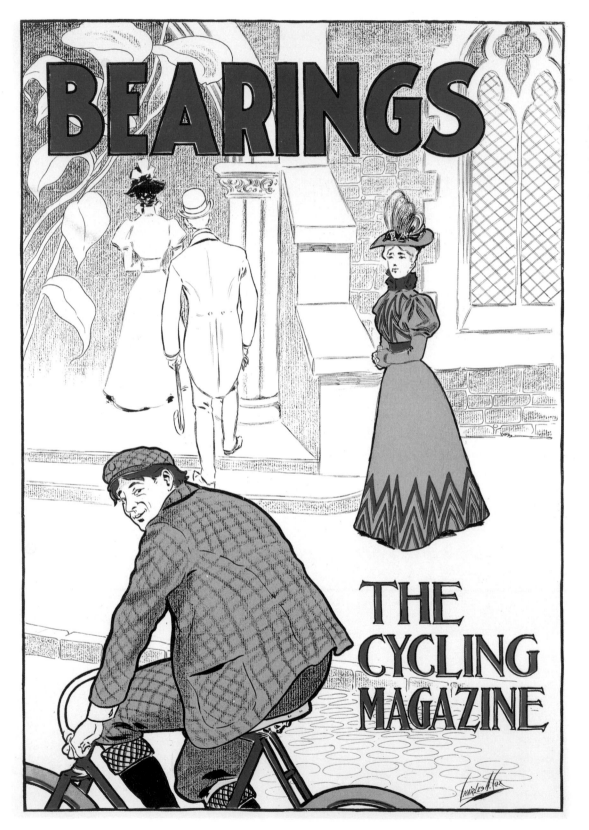

46. CHARLES ARTHUR COX

Bearings Magazine (Chicago). *Bearings.* c. 1895. Color lithograph, 17¾ x 12½ in. (45 x 31.8 cm). National Museum of American Art, Smithsonian Institution, museum purchase.

Cox designed a number of posters for *Bearings,* a fashionable magazine for bicycle enthusiasts of the 1890s.

47. MAXFIELD PARRISH

The Adlake Camera. 1897.
Color lithograph, 11 x 17 in.
(27.9 x 43.1 cm). Alan and
Lois Fern.

Around the turn of the century, Parrish designed posters, illustrated books, and worked increasingly for major companies like Adlake Cameras. Here he presents the camera with both its subject and its user comfortably seated and at ease with the equipment. Although early forms of photography were announced and patented in the 1830s, box cameras like the one shown here were quite new in 1897.

48. MAXFIELD PARRISH

Harper & Brothers (New York). *Harper's Weekly.* 1897. Photographic lithograph, 18¾ x 14 in. (46.7 x 35.5 cm). Virginia Museum of Fine Arts.

The Industrial Revolution brought technological advances in photoengraving and printing machinery, which offered designers more influence over the aesthetic quality of the printed image. Parrish's stylish poster is an example of these advances and the increased prosperity that many Americans enjoyed in the late nineteenth century. It was the combination of new technology and economic growth that fueled the poster craze of the 1890s.

49. MAXFIELD PARRISH

The Century Co. (New York),
printed by The Thomas & Wylie
Lithographic Co. *The Century
Midsummer Holiday Number.*
1897. Color lithograph,
18⁹⁄₁₆ x 12 in. (47.1 x 30.6 cm).
Delaware Art Museum, gift of
Mrs. J. Marshall Cole.

Produced as an entry for
an 1896 *Century* magazine
poster contest, this appealing work by the young
Maxfield Parrish was
awarded second prize.
Parrish's designs, often featuring lush settings and
female nudes, were pro-
duced for a wide variety of
magazines and other com-
mercial products. Poster
and calendar illustrations
by Parrish were widely
displayed in homes at the
turn of the century.

50. FREDERIC WINTHROP RAMSDELL

American Crescent Cycles.
1899. Color lithograph,
65 x 44 in. (165.1 x 111.8 cm).
Steven Schmidt.

52. NORMAN ERICKSON

William R. Crawford Lithography. *Steel Mills at Gary by South Shore Line.* 1928. Color lithograph, 41¾ x 28 in. (106 x 71.1 cm). Chicago Historical Society.

The proliferation of railroad lines across the country made travel, whether to natural spectacles of the American West like Yellowstone and Yosemite, or to industrial wonders like the steelworks on Chicago's South Side, a popular leisure pursuit.

53. JACK RIVOLTA

WPA, New York Federal Art Project. *Up Where Winter Calls to Play.* 1936–41. Color silkscreen, 25 x 16.5 in. (63 x 42 cm). Library of Congress, Prints and Photographs Division.

One of the themes promoted by the Works Progress Administration in its writers' and artists' projects was the rediscovery of American regional landscapes. At the same time, New Deal agencies exhorted Americans to exercise and to engage in outdoor activity in an effort to improve public health. Rural New York State, with its facilities for winter recreation and sport, offered a wholesome antidote to urban environments.

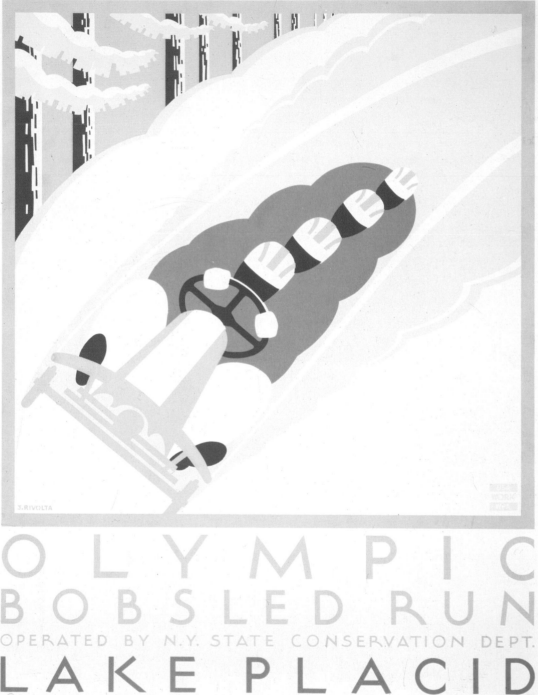

You don't have to be Jewish

to love Levy's
real Jewish Rye

54. WILLIAM TAUBIN (ART DIRECTOR) AND HOWARD ZIEFF (PHOTOGRAPHER)

You Don't Have to Be Jewish to Love Levy's. 1967. Offset lithograph, 45 x 29½ in. (114.3 x 75 cm). Collection of Mr. Jack Rennert, New York City.

55. LANCE HIDY

Meriden-Stinehour. 1982. Offset lithograph and letterpress, two panels, each 30 x 10 in. (76.2 x 25.4 cm). Alan and Lois Fern.

Hidy has said, "From an artistic standpoint, poster design is far more challenging than commercial book design, primarily because I can work with color, composition, metaphoric imagery, and letter forms to represent a complex thought in minimal visual terms . . . . Furthermore, I can do the work privately, without artistic supervision from a publishing committee." Hidy's early experience working for Roderick Stinehour, a respected commercial printer located in Vermont, offered an opportunity to learn a great deal about the technical possibilities and limitations of offset printing.

56. APRIL GREIMAN

The Pikes Peak Lithographing Co. 1992. Offset two-sided lithograph, 45 x 44 in. (114.3 x 111.8 cm). April Greiman.

For the Pikes Peak Lithographing Co., Greiman combined contemporary computer graphics with a distinctive composition, organized around abstract fields of color. This two-sided large-format sheet suggests the specialty of the printing company.

57. DAVID LANCE GOINES

Chez Panisse Café & Restaurant, Twenty-First Birthday. 1992. Photo-offset lithograph, 24 x 17½ in. (60.9 x 44.4 cm). Todd Padgett, Louvre, San Francisco.

CHEZ PANISSE
CAFÉ & RESTAURANT
TWENTY-FIRST BIRTHDAY
1517 SHATTUCK AVENUE · BERKELEY · CALIFORNIA · 94709 & 510·548·5525

58. ROBERT PISANO AND RANDY O'BREZAR (PHOTOGRAPHERS)

Boeing 777. 1994. Mechanical reproduction, 24 x 34 in. (61.1 x 86.4 cm). National Museum of American Art, Smithsonian Institution, gift of The Boeing Company.

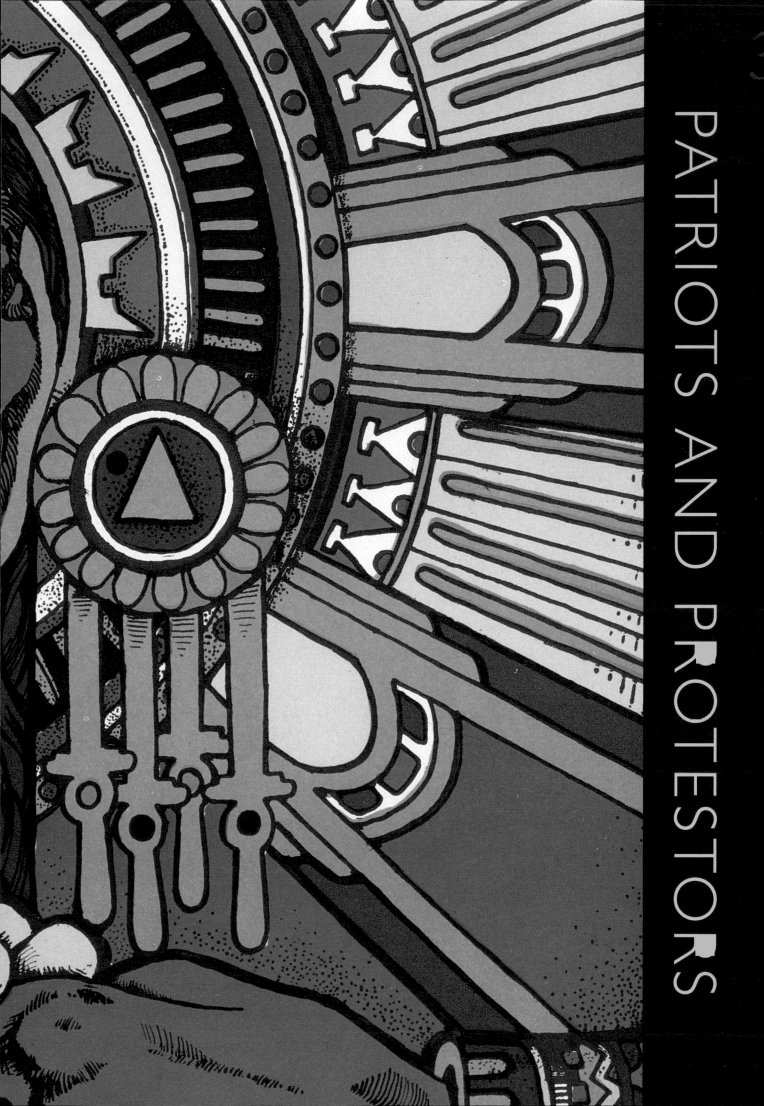

PATRIOTS AND PROTESTORS

60. JAMES MONTGOMERY FLAGG

I Want You for U.S. Army. 1917. Color lithograph, 39½ x 29⅛ in. (100.4 x 73.8 cm). National Museum of American Art, Smithsonian Institution, gift of Barry and Melissa Vilkin.

Used for recruitment during World War I, and again during World War II, Flagg's popular poster demonstrates the commanding effectiveness of a strong design and simple message.

61. JOSEPH PENNELL

That Liberty Shall Not Perish from the Earth – Buy Liberty Bonds. c. 1917. Lithograph, 40¾ x 28¼ in. (103.5 x 71.8 cm). National Museum of American Art, Smithsonian Institution, gift of Barry and Melissa Vilkin.

Best known as an illustrator, Joseph Pennell worked in a style of line drawing already familiar to many from the work of James Abbott McNeill Whistler, whose style captured the energy of light. Pennell creates a landscape of liberty endangered – almost destroyed – in this rosy-hued poster. The need for freedom, so valued by the artists of the day, is articulated here in support of the Liberty Loan bond drive.

62. CHARLES DANA GIBSON

Help Her Carry On! "Miss America Reports for Service, Sir." 1917–18. Offset lithograph, 42 x 28 in. (106.7 x 71.1 cm). Library of Congress, Prints and Photographs Division.

When war preparations were beginning, Gibson and his fellow illustrators volunteered to design posters for government agencies. We know Gibson's name primarily for his "girls," and this Miss America is a properly feminine character, ready to do her part for the military by helping with traditional, limited "woman's duties," such as running social clubs.

63. EDWARD PENFIELD

Y.W.C.A. *The Girl on the Land Serves the Nation's Need.* 1917–18. Color lithograph, 25 x 30 in. (76.2 x 63.5 cm). Hoover Institution Archives, Stanford University.

The dramatic image Penfield made for the Young Women's Christian Association late in his career exemplifies his use of flattened shapes and bold composition. In contrast with his early work, here he reduces the decorative elements and focuses on the broad planes of color to make silhouettes of the figures carrying a hoe, a rake, and harvested vegetables. Despite their competence with tools and farm animals and their khaki-colored uniforms that evoke thoughts of the boys gone off to war, these "girls" remain feminine in face and manner.

64. HOWARD CHANDLER CHRISTY

If You Want to Fight! Join the Marines. 1918. Color lithograph, 40 x 30 in. (101.6 x 76.2 cm). Library of Congress, Prints and Photographs Division.

Historian Jordan A. Schwarz wrote that "the heroes of the Great War were its administrators of the home front...ingenious organizers, managers and publicists of 1917–1918 [who] rallied an unenthusiastic American citizenry to arms in support of a dubious European adventure...." Posters such as Christy's were essential to this campaign and helped to solidify the nation's resolve to sustain a military-industrial effort of unprecedented scale.

65. CHARLES LIVINGSTON BULL

U.S. Food Administration. *Save the Products of the Land: Eat More Fish – They Feed Themselves.* 1918. Offset lithograph, 30 x 20 in. (76 x 51 cm). National Museum of American History Archives Center.

66. JEAN CARLU

Division of Information, Office
for Emergency Management
(Washington, D.C.). *America's
Answer! Production.* 1942.
Offset lithograph, 30 x 40 in.
(76.2 x 101.6 cm). National
Museum of American Art,
Smithsonian Institution, gift
of Barry and Melissa Vilkin.

This is the Enemy

WINNER R. HOE & CO., INC. AWARD — NATIONAL WAR POSTER COMPETITION
HELD UNDER AUSPICES OF ARTISTS FOR VICTORY, INC. — COUNCIL FOR DEMOCRACY — MUSEUM OF MODERN ART
REPRODUCED THROUGH COURTESY OF R. HOE & CO., INC., NEW YORK, N.Y.   R. HOE & CO., INC.   LITHOGRAPHED IN U.S.A. ON HOE SUPER-OFFSET PRESS BY GRINNELL LITHOGRAPHIC CO., NEW YORK, N.Y.

67. KARL KOEHLER AND VICTOR ANCONA

This Is the Enemy. 1942. Offset lithograph, 34 x 24 in. (86.5 x 61 cm). National Museum of American Art, Smithsonian Institution, gift of Barry and Melissa Vilkin.

At the start of the United States's involvement in World War II, the Roosevelt administration felt the need to counter the powerful antiwar messages of such media figures as newspaper magnate William Randolph Hearst and radio personality Father Coughlin. Karl Koehler and Victor Ancona's portrayal of a sinister Nazi officer echoes Roosevelt's characterization of the Axis powers as gangsters, bandits, and criminals.

68. J. HOWARD MILLER

Westinghouse for War
Production Coordinating
Committee. *We Can Do It!*
c. 1942. Photolithograph,
22 x 17 in. (55.9 x 43.2 cm).
National Archives,
Washington, D.C.

69. LAWRENCE B. SMITH

Don't Let That Shadow Touch Them. 1942. Offset lithograph, 40 x 28½ in. (101.6 x 72.4 cm). National Museum of American Art, Smithsonian Institution, gift of Barry and Melissa Vilkin.

70. UNKNOWN

General Cable Corporation. *Are You Doing All You Can?* 1942. Photomechanical lithograph, 28 x 22 in. (71.1 x 55.9 cm). National Museum of American History, Smithsonian Institution, gift of General Cable Corporation.

71. UNKNOWN

Women in Industry . . . We Can't Win without Them. c. 1942. Collage on board with tempera paint and photographic elements, 12 ½ x 15 ⅞ in. (38.7 x 40.4 cm). National Archives, Washington, D.C.

72. BEN SHAHN

The Progressive Party (New York).
A Good Man Is Hard to Find
(depicting Truman and Dewey).
1948. Color lithograph,
45 ½ x 30 in. (115.6 x 76.2 cm).
Collection Merrill C. Berman.
© 1998 Estate of Ben Shahn/
Licensed by VAGA, New York, N.Y.

73. BEN SHAHN

CIO Political Action Committee. *Break Reaction's Grip – Register – Vote.* 1946. Offset lithograph, 41¼ x 29 in. (104.8 x 73.7 cm). Leslie, Judy, and Gabri Schreyer, and Alice Schreyer Batko. © 1998 Estate of Ben Shahn/Licensed by VAGA, New York, N.Y.

Shahn, noted for such paintings as *The Passion of Sacco and Vanzetti,* in which he expressed his reaction to an important and notorious case in American justice, was a remarkably effective photographer working for the Farm Security Administration in the 1930s. Increasingly in the 1940s, he also worked as an inspired postermaker. The immediacy of his drawing and his fervent messages for progressive causes and union issues define a substantial body of work. His designs are instantly recognized for their figurative style, strong outlines, and bright color planes.

74. ROCKWELL KENT

Save This Right Hand. 1949. Color lithograph, 15½ x 11 in. (39.4 x 27.9 cm). The Eliot H. Stanley Collection, Portland, Maine.

Eliot Stanley, who collected this poster, remarked: "The 'right hand' of the ILWU was in particular Harry Bridges; his conviction for perjury, which this poster addresses metaphorically, was eventually overturned by the U.S. Supreme Court in 1953. Kent's poster is a model of the genre: strong metaphor, immediacy, clarity, simplicity, and gut-level communication – so graphic that it makes those who work with their hands wince."

75. SEYMOUR CHWAST

End Bad Breath. 1967. Offset lithograph, 37 ¹³⁄₁₆ x 25 ³⁄₁₆ in. (96 x 63.9 cm). The Pushpin Group.

Chwast (pronounced "kwast") says that he begins every project as a design with an illustration. In *End Bad Breath*, the drawing flashes the message in a bright, unexpected, new way.

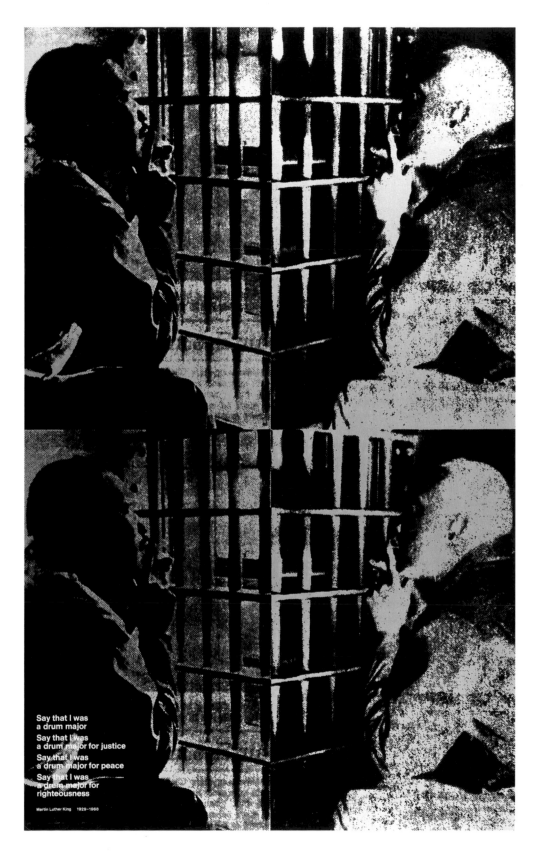

76. PETER GEE

Martin Luther King, Jr. 1968
Photo silkscreen on foil paper
30 x 19 in. (76.2 x 48.3 cm).
Mary Haskell.

Peter Gee's juxtaposition
of positive and negative
photographic images of
Martin Luther King, Jr.
suggests a visual commen-
tary on public perception
of the slain civil rights
leader during his lifetime.
Jailed repeatedly for leading nonviolent protests
against racist policies and
practices during the 1960s,
here King appears to be
looking beyond the prison
bars in a moment of quiet,
personal reflection.

77. UNKNOWN

Girls Say Yes to Boys Who Say No. c. 1968. Photomechanical lithograph, 42 x 29½ in. (106.7 x 74.9 cm). National Museum of American History, Smithsonian Institution, gift of William Mears.

This antidraft poster features singer and activist Joan Baez (left) with her sisters.

who has a better right to oppose the war?

to send contributions and for information, write:
student mobilization committee to end the war in vietnam
857 broadway, new york city 10003. (212) 675-8465

78. RICHARD AVEDON

Student Mobilization Committee to End the War in Vietnam (New York). *Who Has a Better Right to Oppose the War?* 1969. Offset lithograph, 37⅘ x 24 in. (96 x 61 cm). Library of Congress, Prints and Photographs Division.

79. R. L. HAEBERLE (PHOTOGRAPHER) AND PETER BRANDT (DESIGNER)

Art Workers Coalition. *Q: And Babies? A: And Babies.* 1970. Offset lithograph, 25 x 38 in. (63.5 x 96.5 cm). Mary Haskell.

And Babies? is an outcry against the brutal slaughter of war. It was first produced during the antiwar movement of the Vietnam years, after the slaying at My Lai. That massacre was the catalyst for a broad-based protest voiced by an underground, alternative, liberal, youth-oriented, and counter-culture media. Despite the refusal of the client museum to pay for the poster as originally planned, the force of the image has marked it as a universal classic protest against war.

FREE THE NEW YORK PANTHER 21

POWER TO THE PEOPLE

The Committe to Defend the Panther 21
37 Union Square West, 4th Floor
New York, New York 10003
243-7560

ARM

80. UNKNOWN

The Committee to Defend
the Panther 21. *Power to the
People.* 1970. Photographic
silkscreen, 40½ x 29½ in.
(102.9 x 74.9 cm). National
Museum of American History,
Smithsonian Institution, gift
of Jane Griffin and William H.
Yeingst.

81. IVAN CHERMAYEFF

Department of the Interior, National Park Service. *Visit the American Museum of Immigration at the Statue of Liberty.* 1974. Mechanical reproduction, 42 x 28 in. (106.7 x 71.1 cm). National Museum of American Art, Smithsonian Institution.

Visit the American Museum of Immigration at the Statue of Liberty

Statue of Liberty National Monument, New York, New York U.S. Department of the Interior, National Park Service

I pledge allegiance to the flag of the United States of America and to the republic for which it stands, indivisible, with liberty and justice for all.

82. RON BOROWSKI (PHOTOGRAPHER)

Starfish Publications. *I Pledge Allegiance.* 1970. Offset lithograph, 28 x 22 in. (71.1 x 55.9 cm). Mary Haskell.

Borowski's compelling image was first used by graphic artist Louis Dorfsman to create a newspaper advertisement for the 1968 CBS television series *Of Black America.* It was later designed as a poster with the addition of the text "I pledge allegiance," effectively underscoring the ambivalence in this man's face.

83. RUPERT GARCÍA

No More o' This Shit. 1969. Color silkscreen, 24 x 18 in. (61 x 45.9 cm). Achenbach Collection, The Fine Arts Museums of San Francisco, California.

Rupert García called attention to the all-too-prevalent stereotyping of minorities in advertisements when he turned a familiar scene – serving a bowl of cereal – into a poster that clearly points to a subversive irony. The use of brilliant color and flat design also links him to a long tradition of Mexican propaganda posters.

NO MORE O' THIS SHIT.

84. J. GOKEY

This Is How the White Man's Law Fits the Indian. 1972. Photomechanical lithograph, 24½ x 16 in. (62.2 x 40.7 cm). National Museum of American History, Smithsonian Institution, gift of Edith P. Mayo.

"This Is How the White Man's Law Fits the Indian"

After the Treaty of Cedars, in 1836, Chief Oshkosh was presented with a top hat and formal dress coat. Appreciating the irony of this incongruous gift, upon the occasion of the Indians being forced to cede much of their land, Oshkosh paraded before the Indians to say, "Don't I look awful? This is the way the white man's law fits the Indian."

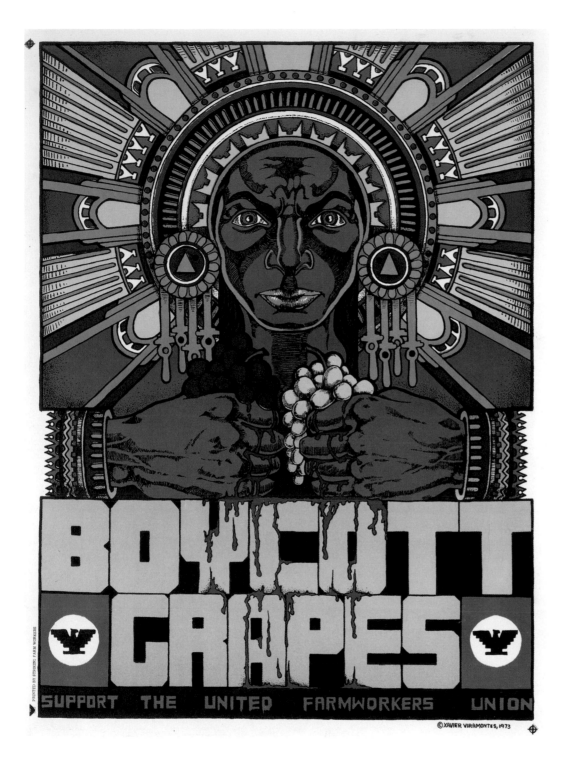

85. XAVIER VIRAMONTES

Printed by striking farmworkers.
Boycott Grapes: Support the United Farm Workers Union.
1973. Offset lithograph,
23 ⅝ x 17 ⅝ in. (60 x 44.6 cm).
National Museum of American Art, Smithsonian Institution, gift of Tomás Ybarra-Frausto.

Xavier Viramontes recounted his memories of the grape boycott and the design of this poster: "The idea behind the making of the poster was to help the farmworkers in their struggle with the grape growers and encourage people to continue the boycott. Up to that point, there were no strong images associated with the boycott, since most of the other posters used by the Farm Workers Union were mostly type. . . . I decided that a strong image was needed – a strong brown image. So, I went with the idea of using a dark-brown Aztec god-like figure with the blood of grapes dripping through his fingers. The image itself conveys the message, the lettering serves to underline the message."

Do women have to be naked to get into the Met. Museum?

Less than **5%** of the **artists** in the Modern Art Sections are women, but **85%** of the **nudes** are female.

GUERRILLA GIRLS Box 1056 Cooper Sta. NY, NY 10276
CONSCIENCE OF THE ART WORLD

86. GUERRILLA GIRLS

Do Women Have to Be Naked to Get into the Metropolitan Museum? 1989. Various materials, 11¼ x 28⅜ in. (28.6 x 72.1 cm). Falkirk Cultural Center.

With humor, irony, and the power of anonymity, the ape-masked Guerrilla Girls and their posters have spoken out against sexism and racism in the New York art world since the mid-1980s. One of their tactics, which has been successful in the sense that it has caused real change, has been to publicize the names of fine art galleries and museums that do not, or do not frequently, exhibit works by women or people of color. Similar activist groups have been formed in San Francisco (Guerrilla Girls West), Austin, Boston, Chicago, Louisville, Los Angeles, Minneapolis, Tampa, and Washington, D.C.

87. ESTER HERNANDEZ

Sun Mad Raisins. 1982.
Serigraph, 22 x 17 in.
(55.9 x 43.2 cm). National
Museum of American Art,
Smithsonian Institution, gift
of Tomás Ybarra-Frausto.

At first glance this poster
seems to present the familiar image of a popular
product, but then Ester
Hernandez's smiling skele-
ton grape picker emerges.
The artist warns of the
health hazards to farm-
workers from contami-
nated water. This is only
one of the many issues
Hernandez has exposed
through her involvement
with Latina women and
their lives in America.

88. LISA EMMONS

New York Mobilization for
Survival. *And Then There
Was Nothing.* c. 1974 Photo-
mechanical lithograph, 24 ½ x
20⅛ in. (81.1 x 62.3 cm).
National Museum of American
History, Smithsonian Institution,
gift of Anne B. Zill.

4

EARTh

89. LESTER BEALL

Light from the series "Rural Electrification Administration." 1937. Lithograph, 40 x 30 in. (101.6 x 76.2 cm). Lester Beall Collection, Wallace Library, Rochester Institute of Technology.

The Rural Electrification Administration, a division of the Department of Agriculture, was developed by President Franklin Delano Roosevelt to improve the nation's rural areas as well as to revive the post-Depression economy by providing jobs. As one of the first graphic designers to work on this project, Lester Beall created a series of posters for the administration from 1937 to 1941. Because the audience for these posters had limited reading skills, these simple but visually dramatic posters express their messages in primarily graphic terms. The vivid design also reflects the influence of Russian Constructivists on Beall's style. The success of the poster series boosted Beall's career and became a benchmark in the history of graphic design.

ESKIMO MASK · WESTERN ALASKA

INDIAN COURT
FEDERAL BUILDING
GOLDEN GATE INTERNATIONAL EXPOSITION
SAN FRANCISCO 1939

90. LOUIS B. SIEGRIEST

Eskimo Mask . . . Western Alaska. 1939. Serigraph, 36⅛ x 25¼ in. (91.6 x 64 cm). National Museum of American Art, Smithsonian Institution, gift of Ralph H. Lewis.

When San Francisco celebrated the Golden Gate International Exposition in 1939, this poster was one of the eight-piece "Indian Court" series by Louis Siegriest. The artist chose images representing many tribal nations using materials given to him by the Bureau of Indian Affairs. The silkscreening was done by the Works Project Administration and supervised by Siegriest on a boat anchored off Treasure Island, the location of the exposition.

91. ALBERT M. BENDER

Federal Art Project (Chicago). *Jobs for Girls & Women.* 1941. Color silkscreen on board, 22 x 14 in. (55.9 x 35.6 cm). Library of Congress, Prints and Photographs Division.

Educating young people was an important goal of the social planners who proposed the National Youth Association. The Works Progress Administration's Federal Art Project created strong graphic designs with powerfully communicative images in large editions, effectively informing the public of the opportunities for paid work.

92. UNKNOWN

She's Helping . . . What Are You Doing? c. 1942. Pencil drawing, 17 x 15 ¼ in. (45.1 x 38.7 cm). National Archives, Washington, D.C.

93. UNKNOWN

If You Don't Need It . . . Don't Buy It! c. 1942. Graphite, blue pencil, and blue tempera paint, 20 x 13 ⅝ in. (50.8 x 34.5 cm). National Archives, Washington, D.C.

This is America..

Courtesy Farm Security Administration   *Photo By Lange

Where a fellow can start on the home team and wind up in the big league. Where there is always room at the top for the fellow who has it on the ball ★ This is _your_ America!

...Keep it Free!

Copyright 1942 - The Sheldon-Claire Co.
520 North Michigan Ave., Chicago

Lithographed in U. S. A.   Form No. 11

95. DOROTHEA LANGE

Where a Fellow Can Start on the Home Team and Wind Up in the Big League, from the series "This Is America." 1942. Photomechanical lithograph, 36 x 24 in. (91.4 x 61 cm). The National Museum of American History, Smithsonian Institution, gift of the Sheldon-Claire Company.

After her seminal work for the Farm Security Agency and her development of documentary standards as applied to rural conditions in the United States in the 1930s, Dorothea Lange went on to work for other government projects. The appropriation of original black-and-white photographs for color images became common practice for her photographs in the public domain.

Here the sentiment about "big league" opportunity might have been a quotation from a participant. Lange and her husband, Paul Taylor, a labor economist, both believed that social programs could change the lives of ordinary Americans.

96. NORMAN ROCKWELL

Save Freedom of Speech. 1943.
Color lithograph, 40 x 28½ in.
(101.6 x 72.4 cm). Hoover
Institution Archives, Stanford
University.

In a historic address before
the Congress on January 6,
1941, President Franklin
D. Roosevelt described the
"unprecedented" threat
that Nazi domination of
Europe presented to
American security. In doing
so, he appealed directly to
core beliefs that Americans
hold about the freedoms of
speech and worship, as
well as the freedoms to
fight against fear and want.
Norman Rockwell offered
to produce a series of four
paintings with American
scenes to illustrate the
"Four Freedoms." First distributed by *The Saturday
Evening Post*, the posters
were later effectively used
by the U.S. government to
sell war bonds.

YOU HAVE NOT CONVERTED A MAN BECAUSE YOU HAVE SILENCED HIM

(John, Viscount Morley, On Compromise, 1874)

Ben Shahn

Great Ideas of Western Man... one of a series **CCA** Container Corporation of America

97. BEN SHAHN

Container Corporation of America. *You Have Not Converted a Man Because You Have Silenced Him.* 1968. Offset lithograph, 45 x 30 in. (114.2 x 76.2 cm). National Museum of American Art, Smithsonian Institution, gift of the Container Corporation of America. © 1998 Estate of Ben Shahn/Licensed by VAGA, New York, N.Y.

In this poster, Shahn brings his distinctive style of creating a figure with black crayon line into balance with his extensive interest in lettering and typography. It was produced as part of the "Great Ideas of Western Man" series issued by the Container Corporation of America. Here Shahn illustrates a quotation from John Viscount Morley, an English Member of Parliament and Secretary of State of India. This poster joins an artist known for his liberal views with a politician remembered as an outspoken pacifist.

98. ERIK NITSCHE

New York Subway Association.
Say it Fast. . .Often. . . in Color.
1947. Offset lithograph,
45 ¼ x 29 ½ in. (114.9 x 74.9 cm).
Collection Merrill C. Berman.

99. JAMES D. ROSE

The Last Redwoods – Sierra Club. 1967. Color offset lithograph, 37 ½ x 25 ¼ in. (95.3 x 64.1 cm). The Oakland Museum of California, gift of William E. Colby Memorial Library, Sierra Club.

When you've seen one redwood stump, you've seen them all.

Beautiful, weren't they?

Photographs by JAMES D. ROSE

THE LAST REDWOODS

Some of the most beautiful redwood forest ever seen was still living in 1966 in the headwaters of the North Fork of Lost Man Creek, part of the Redwood Creek watershed owned by Arcata Redwood Company.

Now the beauty has vanished forever. The small photographs shows what was lost. The forest was cut down in 1967.

If established soon, a national park can rescue the best redwood forest that still lives. Failing that, continued logging will leave only stumpland outside the scattered state redwood parks.

Following a proposal by the National Park Service, most major conservation groups in the country have endorsed a national park in Redwood Creek.

Much of the forest is gone today because the public and the Congress did not know what was being lost. There is still just enough time, though, to save the remainder of this unsurpassed scenic resource —the greatest redwood forest left on earth.

Copyright, August 1967, by the Sierra Club.   *IN THE SIERRA CLUB EXHIBIT FORMAT SERIES*

100. TOMI UNGERER

Black Power/White Power. 1967.
Offset lithograph, 28 x 20 in.
(71 x 51 cm). Mary Haskell.

Ungerer explains his
incisive view of racial situa-
tions: "I'm just a specta-
tor," he says of his work,
"and I draw what I see and
make my comments. Some
of my books are nice, some
are aggressive and despair-
ing. We have all of these
elements in us and I use all
of them." From the heart
of the civil rights move-
ment, he ironically depicts
the gulf between activists as
each devours the other.

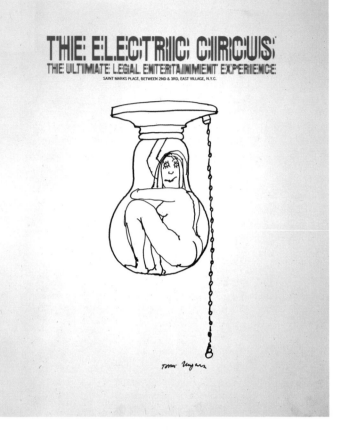

101. TOMI UNGERER

The Electric Circus (New York). *The Electric Circus – The Ultimate Legal Entertainment Experience.* 1969. Offset lithograph, 28 x 22 in. (71 x 56 cm). Library of Congress, Prints and Photographs Division.

Among the most prolific of illustrators, Ungerer has devised drawings for irreverent children's books, as well as civil rights and political posters. While he says that he does not believe that art or posters can change people's minds, he continues to make protest and advocacy posters. In his years in the United States after he left war-scarred Europe, he found support for his work as an illustrator in New York City's Jewish community, which offered him commissions and other opportunities.

102. FELICE REGAN

The Graphic Workshop. *Can You Spare a Pint of Blood for Peace?* 1970. Serigraph, 28 ½ x 22 ⅝ in. (80 x 62.5 cm). Anonymous loan.

103. ROY LICHTENSTEIN

H. K. L. Ltd. (New York
and Boston). *Save Our Planet,
Save Our Water*. 1971.
Screenprint on photo-offset
lithograph, 22⅞ x 31⅞ in.
(58.2 x 81 cm). Pace Prints,
New York.

104. GEORGIA O'KEEFFE

Save Our Planet, Save Our Air.
1971. Offset lithograph,
25 x 36 in. (63.5 x 91.5 cm).
Library of Congress, Prints and
Photographs Division.

This image displays
O'Keeffe's abiding interest
in form and perspective. In
this case, a view of Earth
from above the clouds is
accompanied by text that
reads like a prayer. It is one
of a series of six posters
designed by internationally
recognized artists and published by H. K. L. Ltd. and
the Olivetti Corporation in
the 1970s to promote eco-
logical awareness.

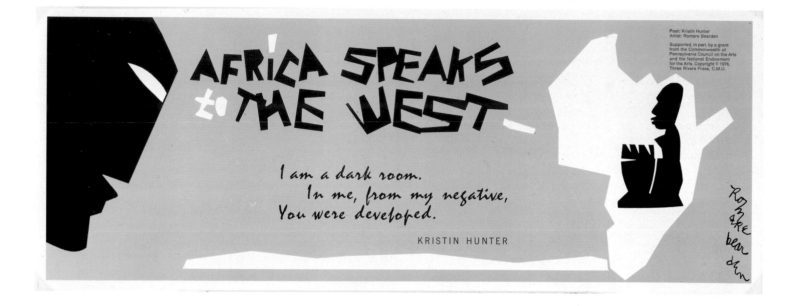

105. ROMARE BEARDEN

Three Rivers Press, Carnegie Mellon University. *Africa Speaks to the West,* from the series "Poetry on the Buses." 1976. Offset lithograph, 11 x 28 in. (27.9 x 71.1 cm). National Museum of American Art, Smithsonian Institution, gift of Poetry on the Buses.

The innovative program, Poetry on the Buses, which began in Pittsburgh, Pennsylvania, commissioned poster designs by nationally recognized artists, who combined their drawings with poetry to enliven mass transportation. Frances Balter, a former member of the Pennsylvania Council on the Arts, founded the group and selected the artists. As a leading African-American painter, Romare Bearden evokes an African sentiment with silhouetted symbols of a drummer and mask, which depict the photographic theme in the poem.

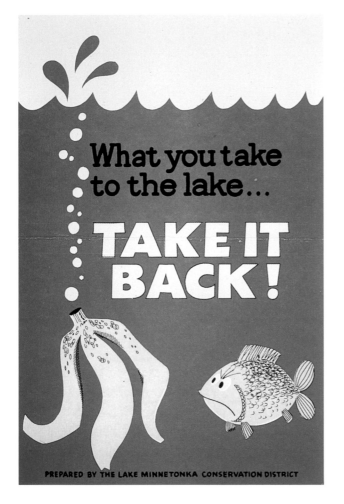

106. ROBERT CONNOLLY

What You Take to the Lake . . . Take It Back! 1977. Color silkscreen, 17¹⁵⁄₁₆ x 11 in. (45.5 x 27.9 cm). Minnesota Historical Society.

Robert Connolly's *Take It Back!* was part of a 1977 environmental awareness campaign sponsored by the Lake Minnetonka Conservation District in Minnesota. Connolly also illustrated a whimsical companion booklet designed to educate the public about the sources of water pollution and the response of the state government. It featured a monster living in the lake happily gorging on sewage, fertilizer runoff, phosphorous, and people's garbage.

107. UNKNOWN

Women's Graphic Collective. *Passivity Is the Dragon.* 1975. Photomechanical lithograph with screened text, 24⅛ x 19 in. (61.3 x 48.4 cm). National Museum of American History, Smithsonian Institution.

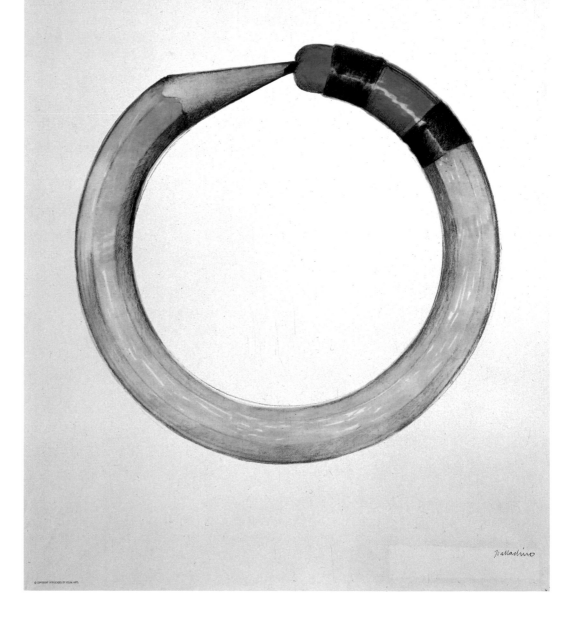

Sitting Bull Previous and eighth as leader of the Sioux at the Battle of the Little Bighorn **Custer Battlefield** National Monument Montana National Park Service U.S. Department of the Interior

109. LEONARD BASKIN

Printed by the Government Printing Office for the National Park Service. *Sitting Bull: Custer Battlefield* (renamed Little Bighorn Battlefield National Monument). 1979. Offset lithograph, 39 x 29⅛ in. (99 x 73.8 cm). National Museum of American Art, Smithsonian Institution, gift of The National Park Service.

110. FELICE REGAN

The Graphic Workshop.
Giant Panda. 1982. Serigraph,
31 ½ x 24 ⅝ in. (80 x 62.5 cm).
The Graphic Workshop.

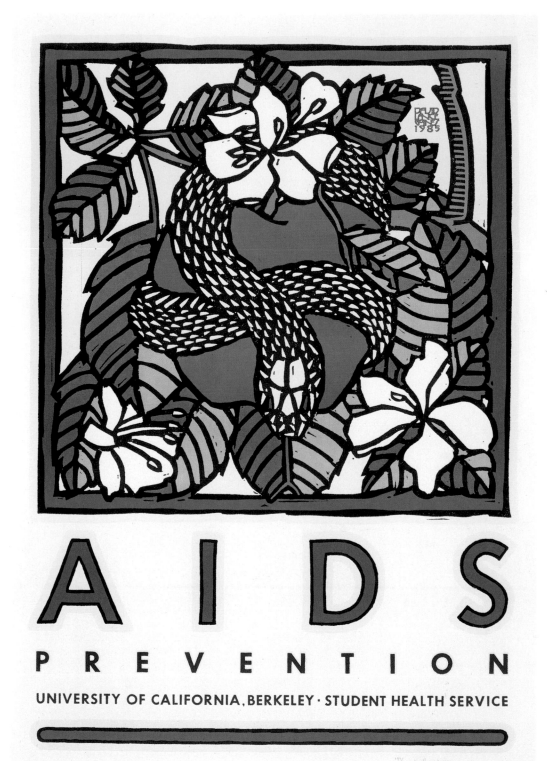

AIDS

PREVENTION

UNIVERSITY OF CALIFORNIA, BERKELEY · STUDENT HEALTH SERVICE

III. DAVID LANCE GOINES

Student Health Service, University of California (Berkeley). *Aids Prevention.* 1985. Photo-offset lithograph, 24 x 17 in. (61 x 43.2 cm). Todd Padgett, Louvre, San Francisco.

Goines explains, "My job is to get your attention and keep it long enough for the message to get across." This poster accomplishes that purpose. It is also a brilliant example of how a large institution deeply concerned for its public image can address a sexual topic in a form suitable for wide public display. Goines's Garden of Eden clearly warns of the danger of AIDS without risking offense.

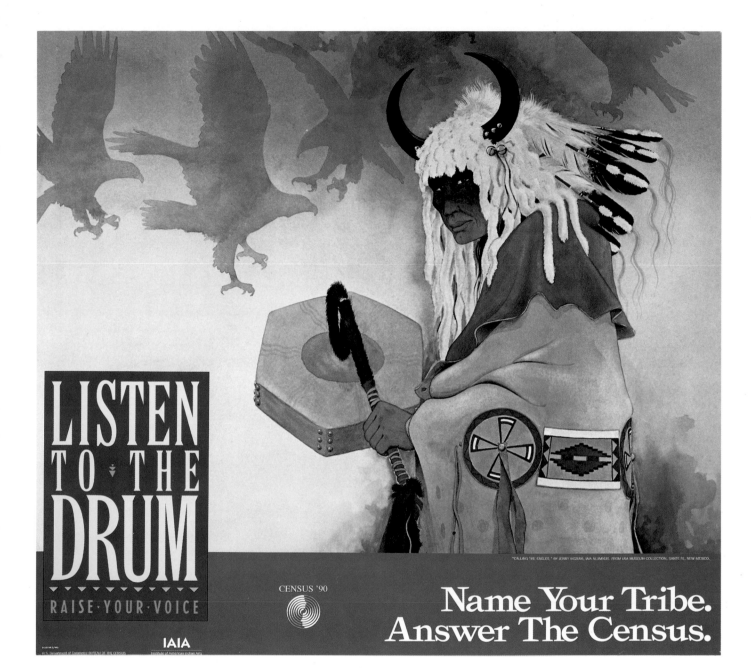

112. JERRY INGRAM

Listen to the Drum: Name Your Tribe. Answer the Census. 1990. Offset lithograph, 21½ x 25 in. (54.6 x 63.5 cm). Bureau of the Census.

113. DOUG MINKLER

Get a Life, Get a Bike. 1993.
Silkscreen print, 13 x 19 in.
(33 x 48.3 cm). Doug Minkler.

For Doug Minkler, making posters "was not about money, making a living, nor beauty, it was for survival . . . a self-defense mechanism." Like many postermakers, Minkler's disagreements with the world around him led him to look for ways to make changes. Though he was trained as a sculptor, he could not find an application for his work in that form that would affect people to the extent he wished. Minkler works on commissioned projects in cooperation with the client or sponsor. In many of his posters he encourages the viewer to take action. To make involvement easy, he usually includes a phone number on the poster itself.

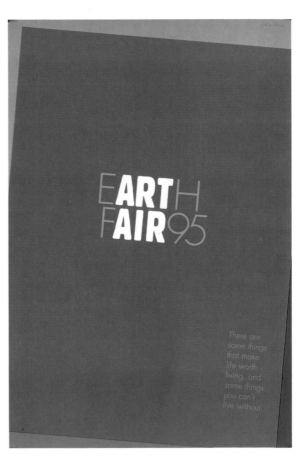

114. MILTON GLASER

Earth Fair (Art Air). 1995.
Mechanical reproduction,
35 ½ x 23 ⅞ in. (90.8 x 60.5 cm).
The Pushpin Group.

Celebrate the twenty-fifth anniversary of Earth Day by making everyday Earth Day.

115. JENNIFER MORLA

Morla Design, Inc. (San Francisco). *Save Our Earth*. 1995. Photomechanical lithograph, 35 ⅛ x 23 ½ in. (89.2 x 59.7 cm). The Pushpin Group.

SPORTS

116. BRISTOW ADAMS

Potomac Press, Washington, D.C. *Mercersburg*. 1903. Photo-lithograph, 22⅖ x 14⅕ in. (57 x 36 cm). Library of Congress, Prints and Photographs Division.

This romantic image of a young ballplayer was created to promote Mercersburg Academy, a preparatory school in Pennsylvania founded in 1893 by Dr. William Mann Irvine. The poster recalls a passion for "America's national game" that grew with industrialization, urbanization, and real increases in leisure time. In 1903 the warring National and American major leagues agreed to a landmark compromise that established a national baseball commission to regulate practices and arbitrate disputes, reinstated the reserve clause limiting players' salaries, and institutionalized the first World Series.

117. OTTO BRENNEMANN

Chicago Lithography Company for the South Shore and South Bend Railroad. *Football: Notre Dame (South Bend).* 1926. Color lithograph, 48 x 42 in. (122 x 106.7 cm). Chicago Historical Society.

118. ALICE NEEL

U.S. Olympic Committee,
Kennedy Graphics, Inc. (New
York). *Olympics 1976*. 1974.
Offset lithograph, 42⅛ x 29⅔ in.
(107 x 64 cm). Library of Con-
gress, Prints and Photographs
Division.

119. KAREN NICOLE MARTIN

Pro Creations Publishing
Company (New Orleans).
1981 Boston Marathon. 1981.
Silkscreen, 28 x 17 in. (71 x
43 cm). Library of Congress,
Prints and Photographs Division.

120. STEPHEN FRYKHOLM

U.S. Ocean Promotion.
*National Offshore Powerboat,
1982 Racing Circuit.* 1982.
Color silkscreen, 39⅖ x 25⅕ in.
(100 x 64 cm). National
Museum of American Art,
Smithsonian Institution, gift
of the artist.

121. RAYMOND SAUNDERS

Knapp Communications
Corporation (Los Angeles).
*Los Angeles 1984 Olympic
Games.* 1982. Offset lithograph,
36⅓ x 24 in. (92 x 61 cm).
Library of Congress, Prints and
Photographs Division.

One of the challenges of
illustrating sporting events
has been to convey move-
ment and speed in a still
image. For Raymond
Saunders, painter and collage artist who combines
found objects on large can-
vases of urban scenes, the
use of color is the key to
his success.

Biographies of
the Postermakers

Brief biographies of the postermakers are included except in the few instances that this information could not be located in libraries, electronic sources, or lending institution files.

RICHARD AVEDON (born 1923)

Born in New York City, Richard Avedon studied at the New School for Social Research. One of the best-known photographers in the United States, he began working for *Harper's Bazaar* in 1945 and has published his work in numerous other magazines, such as *Vogue* and *Life*. He has also done extensive advertising work for a wide variety of commercial firms, including Chanel, General Motors, and Procter & Gamble. Much of Avedon's work has been in fashion photography, in which he has been a pioneering creative force. However, he is also known for his direct, emotionally powerful portraits of some of this century's most important public figures, from Andy Warhol to Dwight D. Eisenhower.

These portraits often show the subject bathed in a blanketing white light with little or no background, thus eliminating extraneous detail that might detract from an immediate perception of the sitter's attitude. Avedon frequently includes the black outlines of the original negative in his prints, utilizing them as a compositional tool as well as to document the photographer's relationship to his subject. His portraits are enduring symbols of the 1960s both in content and formal terms.

Retrospective exhibitions of Avedon's work have been presented in New York City at the Marlborough Gallery and The Metropolitan Museum of Art, in addition to a solo exhibition at The Museum of Modern Art. In 1958 he was voted one of the world's ten best photographers by *Popular Photography* magazine. Among Avedon's numerous honors is a first-place Clio Award for television advertising in 1974. His contributions to the field of graphic design earned him a Certificate of Excellence from the American Institute of Graphic Arts in 1988.

LEONARD BASKIN (born 1922)

Born in New Brunswick, New Jersey, Leonard Baskin was educated at the New York University School of Applied Arts and, after a stint in the United States Navy, at the New School for Social Research in New York City. Travels in Europe in 1950 and 1951 were also of vital importance to his artistic development. Since his first exhibitions in the early 1950s, Baskin has pursued an active career in illustration, design, and sculpture.

Baskin's work is represented in the collections of major museums in the United States and Europe, including the National Gallery of Art, the Victoria and Albert Museum, and the Whitney Museum of American Art. His graphic art and sculpture have been shown in exhibitions in the United States, England, France, and Austria. He is also the recipient of numerous graphic-design awards, including the Special Medal of Merit from the American Institute of Graphic Arts.

Although sculpture has remained a major part of Baskin's oeuvre, it was through graphic design that he originally gained renown. He has worked extensively with woodcuts, chiefly for book illustration. He is the founder of the Gehenna Press in Massachusetts and has been a major force in the revitalization of small American presses. Baskin's posters and other graphic art are distinguished by a consistently powerful directness in exploring the full range of form and expression.

SAUL BASS (1920–1996)
Saul Bass, a native of New York City, was educated at the Art Students League and then studied with Gyorgy Kepes at Brooklyn College. Bass was enormously influenced by Kepes, from whom he learned the basic elements of design and developed a growing sense of humanism in the visual arts. After working for a number of advertising agencies, Bass established the design consulting firm Saul Bass and Associates in 1952. During his career Bass worked for both major corporations and smaller enterprises and was responsible for some of this century's most enduring emblems, including the AT&T globe logo.

In addition to creating posters and prints, Bass was very active in the field of motion pictures. He designed promotional material for studios and soon began creating on-screen graphic sequences that, like his corporate designs, were innovative advances in the field. Bass also wrote and directed a number of short films and directed the now famous shower scene in the film *Psycho*.

Aside from its widespread public presence, Bass's graphic work has been exhibited in museums throughout the United States and Europe, including The Museum of Modern Art and the Cooper-Hewitt National Design Museum in New York, as well as the Library of Congress in Washington, D.C. The recipient of numerous design awards, Bass was also recognized for his excellence in motion-picture making.

LESTER BEALL (1912–1969)
During his childhood in Chicago, Illinois, Lester Beall's mother encouraged him to draw as a means of creative expression and as a diversion from their family's difficult financial situation. In 1917, Beall began attending Saturday art classes at The Art Institute of Chicago, where his youthful efforts received high praise. Beall continued to draw during high school, where his course work included four years of mechanical drawing classes. This early grounding in technical drawing became an important element of his developing graphic style.

Beall enrolled at the University of Chicago as a science major but switched to art history. Because the school offered no studio courses at that time, Beall supplemented his art history classes with additional life drawing and painting classes at the Art Institute. Upon graduation from the university in 1926, Beall found work as a freelance illustrator in Chicago. During the difficult years of the Depression, Beall continued to take studio art classes at the Art Institute. In addition to the classes, he spent a great deal of time at the museum's library, where he reveled in the avant-garde graphic design of French art magazines.

Exposure to these very modern representations of art, typography, and illustration dramatically changed Beall's artistic vision. He incorporated these influences into his own advertising designs to create the dynamic graphic style for which he is remembered today. The Museum of Modern Art recognized Beall's achievements in 1937 with a solo exhibition, the first time a graphic designer was so honored.

ROMARE BEARDEN (1912–1988)
First a student of George Grosz at the Art Students League in New York, Romare Bearden then studied philosophy at the Sorbonne. Active and accomplished as a jazz and folk musician during the 1940s, Bearden experimented with abstraction when he returned to painting in the 1950s. Bearden and other African-American artists formed a group known as Spiral, which considered the artist's responsibility to the community. He based his illustrations of the daily life and mythology of his people on a style partly derived from the use of photo-projection and collage. This style and Bearden's commitment to African-American themes quickly led to several poster commissions.

Because Bearden's art conveyed the fragmented nature of ordinary life, he was called on to adapt his art to reach out to mass audiences. He participated in the Poetry on the Buses project in Philadelphia, which provided a humanizing element among the largely commercial ads seen on urban transportation. Active and well regarded in the artistic community, Bearden also wrote several books on African-American artists and organized exhibitions. Late in his life he experimented with a new style, adopting the intense colors of the Caribbean landscape, where he and his wife had a home.

JOSEPH BINDER (1898–1972)
Born in Vienna and trained as a painter at the Kunstgewerbeschüle, Joseph Binder's early designs won numerous international competitions that placed his posters in public spaces throughout Europe. A leader in

the emerging field of graphic design, Binder felt that posters were "an expression of contemporary civilization reduced to its simplest forms for instantaneous visual communication." In 1933 Binder was invited to serve as a graphic arts lecturer at The Art Institute of Chicago and within the next few years moved to the United States permanently. He won numerous awards for his poster designs, including national competitions sponsored by New York's Museum of Modern Art, the United States Navy, the United Nations, the Red Cross, and the 1939 New York Worlds Fair.

WILL BRADLEY (1868–1962)

Born in Boston, Will Bradley was largely self-taught as an artist. He began working in a printer's shop at the age of twelve in Ishpeming, Michigan, where his mother had moved in 1874 after the death of his father. This work experience would be important in introducing the young man to the many issues of typesetting, advertising, and layout that would occupy him in the years to come.

Bradley executed a number of designs to promote *The Chap-Book*, a short-lived but important publication based in Chicago. His 1894 design for *Chap-Book*, titled *The Twins,* has been called the first American Art Nouveau poster; this and other posters for the magazine brought him widespread recognition and popularity. In 1895, Bradley founded the Wayside Press in Springfield, Massachusetts, and published a monthly arts periodical, *Bradley: His Book.* He remained an active and important member of the graphic arts world for the rest of his long life.

Bradley was well acquainted with the stylistic innovations of his European counterparts. Like many French artists, he borrowed stylistic elements from Japanese prints, working in flat, broad color planes and cropped forms. He appropriated the whiplash curves of the Art Nouveau movement dominant in Europe at the turn of the century and was influenced by the work of the English illustrator Aubrey Beardsley.

CHARLES LIVINGSTON BULL (1874–1932)

Charles Livingston Bull, one of the most prolific and accomplished American wildlife illustrators, received his artistic training at the Philadelphia Art School. He also worked as a taxidermist and was known as an expert in the field of bird and animal anatomy. Bull often sketched at the Bronx Zoo and traveled widely in search of wildlife subjects. He was a strong advocate of biological protection and preservation, creating many images to arouse public support for endangered species such as the bald eagle. He also illustrated a number of important books, including the first edition of Jack London's *Call of the Wild.* Bull's work appeared in a great many periodicals throughout his career.

Bull brought his skill in animal illustration to poster design. Although committed to wildlife illustration, he was able to adapt his style to the needs of commercial poster design and succeeded in creating some of the most enduring images of the first half of the twentieth century. Among his most famous posters are those made for the Barnum & Bailey circus and his effort during World War I to sell savings stamps. Bull also designed posters for a number of federal departments as part of the war effort.

JEAN CARLU (1900–1997)

Born in Bonnières, France, Jean Carlu came from a family of architects and studied to enter that profession. After an accident at the age of eighteen in which he lost his right arm, Carlu turned to graphic design. His early work reveals a fascination with the angular forms and spatial nuances of Cubism.

As Carlu's work evolved over the next two decades, it continued to show a concern with the geometric shapes of Cubism, but this was manifested in very different ways. Carlu sought to create a symbolic language in which color, line, and content would represent emotional values. His work thus achieved a distinctive, streamlined economy of form, rarely incorporating narrative or illustrative elements.

Carlu spent the years of World War II in the United States, where he executed a number of important poster designs for the government's war effort. Characterized by the same scientific precision of form, these extremely popular designs were well suited to the promotion of industrial efficiency. Both American and international design traditions continue to reflect his influence.

ART CHANTRY (born 1954)

Art Chantry has been making posters since he was fifteen. Among his influences are many forms of "outsider art," such as monster magazines, hot-rod art, and psychedelic culture. He found much inspiration for innovative graphic ideas in an article on Polish posters.

Chantry's sense of design relates to the punk scene in Seattle as he finds himself, with the avant-garde, doing posters for local rock concerts. Chantry has championed what he considers the "subculture" of design, a neglected commercial usage of the industrial trade seen in the tool catalogues of the 1940s and 1950s.

Born in Seattle and raised in Tacoma, Chantry received what he describes as "a very potent taste of what it's like to be poor in a single-parent family." Chantry attended college in Bellingham, Washington. He graduated with a degree in painting but turned to the graphic work that had been his livelihood through his school years. In a curious way, Chantry's ability to look for and reinvent the out-of-fashion, the purposely outside the mainstream international style, has resulted in his being selected for many exhibition and design magazines. Even with the recognition of his peers, he chooses to remain as an outsider, often rejecting work with commercial corporate clients for commissions that allow him to remain on the fringe. As he is now the art director of an alternative Seattle paper, he has the advantage of economic stability with the luxury of working only on projects that interest him.

IVAN CHERMAYEFF (born 1932)
Born in London, Ivan Chermayeff was educated at Harvard University, the Institute of Design in Chicago, and the Yale University School of Art and Architecture. In 1960 he and Tom Geismer founded the design firm Chermayeff and Geismer Associates, based in Cambridge, Massachusetts. Chermayeff has served on numerous important design committees, including the Yale Council Committee on Art, and is a trustee of The Museum of Modern Art in New York and a past president of the American Institute of Graphic Arts.

Influenced by the Bauhaus legacy of utilitarian order, Chermayeff has developed unique approaches to modernist graphic design that have gone beyond what he learned from that German school. As he explains, "I like to incorporate handwriting and the physical practice of putting things down . . . nails, tacks, tape, stickers, and things that hold other things together on a temporary basis. . . . My tendency is to reveal that relationship rather than to disguise it."

Chermayeff's poster designs for civic and cultural organizations and numerous corporate clients, as well as his designs for book jackets, have been exhibited in the United States, Japan, and Europe. Among his many awards are the Industrial Art Medal of the American Institute of Architects and the Gold Medal of the Philadelphia Museum of Art.

HOWARD CHANDLER CHRISTY (1873–1952)
Howard Chandler Christy began his career in the visual arts as a student of painting at the National Academy of Design in New York City, eventually turning chiefly to illustration. His work appeared in a number of magazines and books. These illustrations, as well as his sketches of the Rough Riders during the Spanish-American War, earned Christy considerable public recognition and popularity. Perhaps his most enduring image is the famous "Christy girl," the idealized American woman of the 1910s and early 1920s. Among the works in which she was featured were World War I posters designed to encourage young men to enlist.

Christy also worked extensively in portraiture, producing the likenesses of important figures ranging from politicians to entertainers and members of high society. His work has been featured in numerous exhibitions during and after his lifetime.

SEYMOUR CHWAST (born 1931)
Educated at Cooper Union in New York City, Seymour Chwast was a founding member of the important Push Pin Studios and Push Pin Press. Prolific and versatile, he has executed designs for posters, magazines, commercial logos, and record covers, as well as children's books.

Chwast has been the subject of numerous solo exhibitions, and his work is represented in the permanent collections of The Museum of Modern Art in New York and the Suntory Museum in Osaka. In 1983 he was awarded the Saint-Gaudens Medal for Outstanding Achievement by the Cooper Union and was also elected to the Hall of Fame of the Art Directors Club of New York.

Because of the remarkable diversity of Chwast's talent, his work has had an international influence on designers in various fields. He played a key role in creating Push

Pin Studios's distinctive style, which revived the illustrative elements of earlier art movements such as Art Nouveau. This eclecticism was well suited to the 1960s and 1970s, and his visual humor continues to distinguish Push Pin's efforts.

ROBERT CONNOLLY (1918–1995)

Born in Minnesota, Robert Connolly spent the greater part of his career as an art director at advertising agencies in Minneapolis. An avid watercolorist, he also served as a president of the Midwest Watercolor Society. Connolly volunteered his creative talents to a number of organizations and causes. His *Take It Back!* poster was designed to encourage environmental awareness among schoolchildren and recreational patrons at Lake Minnetonka.

PAUL DAVIS (born 1938)

Paul Davis was born in Centrahoma, Oklahoma, and earned a B.F.A. at the School of Visual Arts in New York City, where he studied on a full scholarship. His teachers included Philip Hays, Robert Weaver, Tom Allen, Robert Shore, Howard Simon, George Tscherny, and Burt Hasen. In 1959 he became an apprentice at Push Pin Studios where he was employed until 1962, when he left to do freelance work. Davis has taught at the School of Visual Arts and the University of Colorado. A painter as well as a graphic and poster artist, he has created a wide range of products, from illustrations for national magazines to book jackets and album covers.

Davis has won acclaim for his *Viva la Huelga* poster supporting Cesar Chavez's United Farm Workers Union and for a series of posters for the New York Shakespeare Festival. In designing the theater posters, Davis first paints a relatively small canvas that functions as a model for the final work. The posters were printed in a three-sheet size (42 x 84 inches) for display in New York subways. The demand for Davis's theater posters – not as advertisements but as collectibles – is met by printing one-sheet versions (23 x 46 inches) that are distributed throughout the country.

Davis does not seem to have been negatively affected by the need to satisfy the clients for his posters. In a published collection of these works, he states, "It is impossible for me anyway to follow a layout or an idea I don't like. Each of these paintings represents a sympathetic working relationship with an art director, editor, or client."

MAYNARD DIXON (1875–1946)

Born in Fresno, California, Maynard Dixon was largely self-taught as an artist. His first sketches were of the Western landscape. In 1893 he attended the Mark Hopkins Institute of Art in San Francisco, but withdrew after only three months. That same year his first illustrations for the *Overland Monthly* appeared, beginning a long association with that periodical.

For the next fifty years Dixon traveled and lived throughout the American West. His illustrations of the people, landscape, and lifestyle of this region won him an enduring place in the history of Western artists. In 1920 Dixon married the noted documentary photographer Dorothea Lange. Her unique vision was certainly an important influence on the development of his own realistic approach. Aside from his magazine illustrations, Dixon was prolific in other media, illustrating novels, painting murals in several cities, and even writing poetry.

ARTHUR WESLEY DOW (1857–1922)

Born in Ipswich, Massachusetts, Arthur Wesley Dow studied art in Paris. Upon returning to the United States, he became an important commercial designer. Although he designed relatively few posters, his works are important in their stylistic innovations.

When Dow returned from Paris he became acquainted with Ernest Fenellosa, curator of Oriental art at the Museum of Fine Arts, Boston; this friendship led him to develop a deep interest in Japanese art. As a result, his own designs incorporated the Japanese linear approach to form as well as broad planes of mass and color. Not merely borrowing the forms and style of Japanese art, Dow sought a synthesis of Western and Eastern art. Landscape was of particular importance to Dow, and he executed a number of works based on studies of nature in Ipswich.

In addition to his accomplishments as an artist, Dow was an important educator. He taught at Pratt Institute and the Art Students League at the turn of the century.

JAMES MONTGOMERY FLAGG (1877–1960)

Born in Pelham Manor, New York, James Montgomery Flagg attended several art schools, including four years spent at the Art Students League in New York City. He was prolific in a number of media but is best remembered for his poster designs.

By the turn of the century, Flagg had created a reputation as a graphic designer and illustrator. When the United States entered World War I, he produced his *I Want You for U.S. Army* poster, which quickly became a household icon and one of the most enduring images of the twentieth century. Although Flagg took the design from an earlier British work, he adapted it in a manner that immediately captured the American imagination.

Flagg is also well known for his many pen-and-ink drawings. Fascinated by the vivacity of the 1920s, he sought to capture the spirit of a prosperous nation in a number of intelligent and witty works from that period. During his career Flagg also executed numerous portraits in oil, ranging from sensitive likenesses of family members to grand renderings of statesmen and celebrities such as Theodore Roosevelt.

STEPHEN FRYKHOLM (born 1942)
After his Peace Corps service in Nigeria in the mid-1960s, Stephen Frykholm earned an M.F.A. degree in 1969 from the Cranbrook Academy of Art. Since 1970 he has been employed as a graphic designer by furniture manufacturer Herman Miller, Inc., of Zeeland, Michigan, and is currently the chief creative officer for its subsidiary, Miller SQA. Frykholm's work has been published in books and periodicals nationally, and he was honored by a 1985 AIGA Design Leadership Award presented to Herman Miller for outstanding contributions to the design field. His posters are included in the permanent collections of The Museum of Modern Art and the Library of Congress and have been exhibited in "Posters for a Picnic" at the Renwick Gallery of the National Museum of American Art in Washington, D.C., "The Modern American Poster" at the Museum of American Art in Tokyo, and "Graphic Design in America: A Visual Language History" at the Walker Art Center in Minneapolis. "I've only a few gray hairs," says Frykholm, "but my wider perspective only seems to make trouble for my colleagues. To me, that means keeping on top of things in my profession, my new job at Miller SQA, and learning faster than ever."

RUPERT GARCÍA (born 1941)
Born in French Camp, California, García came from a family active in both the creation and instruction of folk arts and traditions. After completing his service in the U.S.

Air Force in Indochina, García attended the San Francisco School for the Arts on the G.I. Bill. As his education in art intensified so did his interest in politics. He joined Latino and other minority movements in the Bay Area protesting the disproportionate number of these groups being sent into battle in Southeast Asia.

García has proven himself to be not only one of the most important artists of the last twenty-five years, but an important political force as well. Much of his work has dealt with issues of racism and the mistreatment of Latinos in the United States. His style is direct and powerful; he seeks to be both forceful and readily accessible to a wide audience. Keeping these goals in mind, both García's graphic art and his paintings display a skillful unification of the Mexican traditions of Rivera, Siqueiros and Orozco, with elements learned from European artists and those of the American Pop art movement. García's art has evolved stylistically throughout his career, but he has constantly maintained a strong balance of graphic and "fine art."

García has also played an important role in Latino art scholarship. He holds two M.A. degrees – one in studio art and the other in art history. He is the author of an important thesis on California Chicano muralists and has published essays on a number of different subjects including the work of Frida Kahlo. García's continuing legacy constantly addresses the most important issues of contemporary society, both thematically and stylistically.

PETER GEE (born 1932)
English by birth, Peter Gee has spent his career working in New York City and is the founder of the ApoGee Gallery there. While working in New York in the 1960s, Gee created some of the decade's most characteristic images. These works often dealt with the many controversial issues of the day, including the Vietnam War and the civil rights movement. Gee has executed a variety of public and private commissions throughout his career. His work has been featured in major exhibitions in many cities and museums, including The Museum of Modern Art in New York and the Smithsonian Institution. Gee is also the recipient of numerous design and graphic awards.

CHARLES DANA GIBSON (1867–1944)
Born in Roxbury, Massachusetts, Charles Dana Gibson

attended the Art Students League in New York, studying with Thomas Eakins and Kenyon Cox. Hugely successful at the turn of the century, he left New York from 1905 to 1907 to study painting in France, Spain, and Italy.

Gibson's name is still remembered for its association with the icon he created, the "Gibson girl." This idealized, refined, upper-middle-class woman became so popular that she was featured in stage plays, and her image was printed on a variety of domestic objects. The highest-paid illustrator of his time, in 1904 Gibson accepted a contract from *Collier's Weekly,* which paid him $100,000 for one hundred illustrations over four years. Gibson's illustrations gently satirized public life and mores.

During World War I, as president of the Society of Illustrators, Gibson formed and became head of the Division of Pictorial Publicity under the Federal Committee of Public Information. Through this program, prominent illustrators were recruited to design posters, billboards, and other publicity for the war effort. His involvement with publicity during the war led Gibson to become owner and editor of *Life,* a New York–based magazine filled with short articles and illustrations. In the early 1930s Gibson retired to devote more time to painting.

MILTON GLASER (born 1929)

Born in the Bronx, New York, Milton Glaser graduated from Cooper Union in 1951 and then studied at the Academy of Fine Arts in Bologna on a Fulbright scholarship. In 1957 he was a cofounder, with Seymour Chwast and others, of Push Pin Studios in New York, where he executed designs for record covers, books, and posters. His poster of Bob Dylan is one of the most memorable images of the 1960s, embodying for many people the spirit of that period. Glaser and Push Pin Studios worked in an illustrative, often playful style that offered an alternative to the utilitarian spareness of the Bauhaus tradition brought to the United States by Herbert Bayer and other graphic artists. As Glaser said, "I guess the revolutionary thing we did was to take the position that there is no single voice capable of expressing every idea, that romance is still necessary, ornament is necessary, and simplification is not better than complexity." Glaser has also been extremely active in the publishing field, coproducing the magazine *Push Pin Graphic,* as well as executing numerous magazine designs and serving as design director of the *Village Voice.*

Glaser's work has been featured in important exhibitions in Europe and America and has been acquired for the permanent collections of many museums, including The Museum of Modern Art in New York. He holds a number of honorary doctorates and has received the highest awards in his field, including gold medals from the American Institute of Graphic Arts and the Society of Illustrators.

DAVID LANCE GOINES (born 1945)

Born in Grants Pass, Oregon, David Goines studied at the University of California at Berkeley. Before earning his degree in 1965, he worked as a printer's apprentice. Three years later he founded the Saint Hieronymous Press in Berkeley and has worked there ever since. Goines has created well over one hundred poster designs for commercial clients, as well as for political causes and organizations concerned with AIDS prevention. A political activist, he has championed many of the issues dealt with in his posters. Known for his craftsman's approach to design, Goines is involved in all phases of production, from making ink colors to final printing. His work has been the subject of solo exhibitions and is represented in the permanent collections of numerous museums, including The Metropolitan Museum of Art and the Achenbach Collection of the Fine Arts Museums of San Francisco. He is also the author and publisher of a variety of books.

Goines shares with postermakers of the 1890s an interest in lettering, broad, flat color planes and, at times, the curves of Art Nouveau. His designs often feature an intricate web of pattern and color that is reminiscent of the French painters Edouard Vuillard and Pierre Bonnard. The early-twentieth-century German graphic artist Ludwig Hohlwein has also been an important inspiration. Nonetheless, Goines's rich illustrative style is unique and instantly recognizable, synthesizing elements of earlier designs and his own solutions to graphic challenges.

APRIL GREIMAN (born 1948)

Born in the United States and educated both there and in Europe, April Greiman studied commercial art in high school and earned a B.F.A. degree in 1970 at the Kansas City Art Institute. There she took classes with three

European teachers from the Design School of Basel, which were followed by influential studies at that school in Switzerland in 1970–71.

In 1976, after settling in Los Angeles, Greiman developed a remarkably active career in all aspects of graphic design including many projects for corporations, museums, and workshops on poster design. From the outset Greiman has been involved in the use of new technology in design, multimedia, and the "purely scientific." She is also noted for collaborative work with architects, and for a United States Information Agency (USIA) exchange program in which her work traveled throughout Russia in 1994. Her designs have been recognized in a series of major awards and exhibitions.

RICK GRIFFIN (1944–1991)

Born near Palo Verde, Rick Griffin grew up in the surfing culture of southern California, which had a profound influence on his art. After high school, he worked on the staff of *Surfer* magazine and created the best-known surfing cartoon character of the time, Murphy.

In Los Angeles, Griffin met the Jook Savages, a group of artist-musicians, and took part in the writer Ken Kesey's "Watts Acid Test." In the fall of 1966, along with the Jook Savages, he went to San Francisco and began to create rock posters. His first was for a Jook Savages art exhibition. Organizers for the "Human Be-In" saw the poster in San Francisco and asked him to do a poster for their event held in January 1967. Chet Helms, a producer for the Family Dog (a collective interested in social issues), also saw Griffin's work and asked him to design posters for the dance parties at the Avalon Ballroom. In 1967 Berkeley Bonaparte, a poster distribution agency, began employing artists such as Griffin, giving them an opportunity to create and sell posters not specifically made for concerts.

Combining eclectic typefaces and decorative borders with brilliant colors, Griffin's compositions are complex without being illegible. He introduced diverse, often startling objects into his posters, creating visual-verbal puns and playful references to pop culture.

His later works are powerful and bizarre, concerned with ideas of mortality and continuity. Among his last posters were those produced for the San Francisco–based band The Grateful Dead, which illustrate Griffin's vivid imagination and graphic skill.

ESTER HERNANDEZ (born 1944)

When Ester Hernandez was a child she watched as Chicano farmworkers marched through her hometown of Dinuba, California, and were harassed by other local residents. Despite the danger, her family greeted the workers and their leader, Cesar Chavez. At Grove Street College in Oakland, California, as she learned more about Chicano studies, she turned to the art department in an attempt to find understanding for her anger about the treatment of Latina women. She was disappointed to find only one Chicano teacher who understood her need to be an effective agitator rather than "one of the boys," who would emulate the accepted, abstract New York art style. Eventually Hernandez met and joined Rupert García's classes in San Francisco and was invited to enter a Latina women's art exhibition.

Hernandez's posters have been controversial. She recounts how *Sun Mad* began when she "went home to visit my mother in 1979, reading the articles she saved about water contamination in the *barrio*." After thinking about it for two years, remembering how she had worked as a farmhand, Hernandez focused her anger on the dangers of growing grapes for the raisin industry. "I focused on something personal," Hernandez said. "Slowly I began to realize how to transform the Sun Maid and unmask the truth behind the wholesome figures of agribusiness. *Sun Mad* evolved out of my anger and my fear of what would happen to my family, my community, and to myself."

LANCE HIDY (born 1946)

A native of Portland, Oregon, Lance Hidy began his formal art education in 1964 at Yale University's Jonathan Edwards College. To supplement his education, he worked as an apprentice designer for a Portland graphic arts firm during the summers. He demonstrated his interest in graphic arts with the design and printing of two books (one with his own illustrations) using the college's printing press. After graduation, Hidy received a grant to study with Leonard Baskin, an artist with similar interests in engraving and typographic design, who was teaching at Smith College.

In May of 1969, Hidy joined the Godine Press in Brookline, Massachusetts, where he worked in a variety of roles, including designer and pressman, for the next eighteen months. From there he moved to New Hampshire to work at the *Coos County Democrat,* then owned by the respected printer Roderick Stinehour. In 1974, Hidy went into business as a freelance designer. One of his most noted book designs was for Ansel Adams's *Yosemite and the Range of Light.*

Hidy designed his first poster in 1977. His work is distinguished by his use of flat, solid colors and expressiveness with minimal detail.

JERRY INGRAM (born 1941)
Born in Battiest, Oklahoma, part of the Choctaw nation, Jerry Ingram attended the Institute of American Indian Arts in Sante Fe, New Mexico, before receiving a B.A. degree from Oklahoma State Technical Institute in 1966. By then he was already accepting art commissions and soon began to receive awards for his work. In 1967 he moved to New Mexico, where he has continued to paint while establishing himself as an important graphic designer and illustrator.

Over the last quarter century, Ingram has received awards for his achievements in the visual arts and also for his efforts to expand the understanding and appreciation of Native-American culture. His work was presented in a solo exhibition at the Heard Museum in Phoenix in 1972. The historical accuracy of the forms and details he presents distinguishes his work in both graphic and fine arts.

ROCKWELL KENT (1882–1970)
Born in Tarrytown, New York, Rockwell Kent attended the Columbia University School of Architecture. While there, he also enrolled in night and summer classes at several art schools, studying with distinguished artists such as William Merritt Chase, Robert Henri, Kenneth Hayes Miller, and Abbott Handerson Thayer. Kent worked as an architect for a little over a decade, then moved to Maine and supported himself as a manual laborer while painting. His earliest poster designs date to 1917–18, focusing on the choices and sacrifices that must be made during war. They were reproduced from pen, brush, and ink drawings, but he soon began working with woodcuts. Many of Kent's posters used sophisticated symbolism to convey political messages or support social causes.

Kent's paintings and illustrations of Alaska, Tierra del Fuego, Greenland, and other remote locations he had visited won great popularity. However, not all of the attention he received was positive. He was often denounced for having voted as a socialist and for being affiliated with many causes espoused by communists. Despite his political problems, Kent painted, designed posters, and published six books recounting his travels and family history.

KARL KOEHLER (born 1913) and
VICTOR ANCONA (born 1912)
Karl Koehler and Victor Ancona submitted several entries, including their prize-winning poster *This Is the Enemy,* to the National War Poster Competition held during 1942–43. Sponsored by the Artists for Victory, Inc., the Council for Democracy, and The Museum of Modern Art, New York, the goal of the competition was to assemble persuasive images for war propaganda. Artists were given a choice of eight themes and twenty slogans to use in their designs; over two thousand entries were submitted.

FRANK KOZIK (born 1961)
Frank Kozik grew up in Spain, where he dreamed of becoming a scientist, perhaps an astronaut. When he immigrated to the United States in 1976 his life began to change. He dropped out of school and later, in an attempt to turn things around, he joined the military. He wound up in Austin, Texas, where he discovered punk rock and its engaging culture.

Working as a doorman at a nightclub in Austin, he began producing posters for the featured bands. An article about his work in the *Austin Chronicle* helped him land a job at a large T-shirt shop where he gained technical knowledge of printing processes. "After a year spent doing less than 'cool' designs I took my new found technical knowledge and hit the streets, freelance," states Kozik. He has been creating rock posters ever since that are packed with contrasting images – sometimes bright, engaging and aesthetically pleasing, and other times dark and standoffish.

DOROTHEA LANGE (1895–1965)
Dorothea Lange was determined to be a photographer even before she had a camera. Rather than follow her mother's wishes that she train as a schoolteacher, Lange worked as an apprentice in a series of New York studios,

including that of Arnold Genthe. Her plan to travel around the world in 1919 was thwarted when her money was stolen. Stranded in San Francisco, she soon found work as a photographer and made connections to Bay Area camera clubs. But she found her vision of photography, through which she documented the lives of rural American workers, their families, and living conditions, when she began to see the demonstrations and bread lines of the new poor from her Montgomery Street studio during the 1930s. Together with Paul Taylor, who was soon to be her husband, she produced illustrated reports on migrant camps first for the State of California, and then for the Farm Security Administration in Washington, D.C. Her work in black-and-white was often selected to represent the technical and aesthetic standards of this agency under the direction of Roy Stryker.

ROY LICHTENSTEIN (1923–1997)

Born in New York City, Roy Lichtenstein attended the Art Students League, where he studied with the painter Reginald Marsh. He then attended the School of Fine Arts at Ohio State University, earning his B.F.A. degree in 1946 after serving three years in the U.S. Army stationed in Europe. He received his M.F.A. three years later.

Lichtenstein became a major force in the Pop art movement in the 1960s. In addition to painting, he worked in a number of graphic media. As early as 1950, he won design awards for his prints, many of them made at Tyler Graphics in Mount Kisco, New York. Since the early 1960s his prints have been included in important contemporary graphic art exhibitions throughout the country. A major exhibition of his prints was presented at the National Gallery of Art in Washington, D.C., in 1994.

The mass-produced appearance and process-oriented style of Lichenstein's work make it ideally suited to print- and postermaking. He completed innumerable public and private commissions for museums, film and music festivals, political groups, and the American bicentennial.

FLORENCE LUNDBORG (1871–1949)

Born in San Francisco, Florence Lundborg studied with Arthur F. Matthews and Lucia Matthews at the Mark Hopkins Institute in San Francisco and later studied in Italy and France. In addition to designing posters,

Lundborg painted and illustrated books and magazines. She won a bronze medal for three murals for the Women's Board Tea Room, California Building, at San Francisco's Panama–Pacific Exposition in 1915. She later moved to New York, where she also painted several murals.

Greatly influenced by the Arts and Crafts movement in California, Lundborg believed that woodblock designs had "more of the personality of their inventor than the mechanically produced lithograph [could] possibly have." She frequently cut the blocks for her woodcuts herself, including those for six of her seven posters for *The Lark*, a humor and literary magazine to which she also contributed cover illustrations and articles.

PETER MAX (born 1937)

Shortly after Peter Max was born in Berlin, his family moved to Shanghai, where he spent the first ten years of his life. A visually sensitive child, Max speaks of having been dramatically affected by the world that surrounded him in Shanghai. Particularly evocative was the ritualistic painting in a Buddhist temple near his home, especially its use of long, spontaneous brushstrokes. Just as important were the rich sights and sounds of that city's streets and festivals.

After leaving Shanghai, Max lived for periods of time in the mountains of Tibet and also in Israel and Paris before settling in New York in the early 1950s. He incorporated all of these influences into his art, eventually creating a personal language that has earned him important commissions and exhibitions on three continents.

DOUG MINKLER (born 1940)

An active force in the San Francisco area, Doug Minkler has been making posters focused on a variety of social issues since the 1960s, when he was deeply involved with the Bay Area movement protesting American involvement in the Vietnam War. Since then, his posters have used an illustrative style, at times witty and playful, at times direct and brutally honest, to address a range of concerns, from promoting pacifism and education to protesting pollution, corporate misdeeds, and gender inequity. "My posters are a form of self-defense against the inequality, poverty, and violence we're forced to live under," he states. "The lies, the waste, the hate – these are my enemies."

In addition to his graphics work, Minkler is committed

to innovative education in the Bay Area. "My motivation for teaching is the same as that of a union organizer. The more of us there are, organized and clear-thinking, the harder it is for us to be manipulated," he says.

VICTOR MOSCOSO (born 1936)

Born in Spain, Victor Moscoso was the first of the rock poster artists with academic training and experience. After studying art at Cooper Union in New York City and at Yale University, he moved to San Francisco in 1959, where he attended the San Francisco Art Institute, eventually becoming an instructor there.

At a dance at the Avalon Ballroom in San Francisco, Moscoso saw rock posters and decided that he could "make some money doing posters for those guys." In 1966 he began designing posters for the Family Dog and also produced posters for the Avalon Ballroom. Under his own imprint, Neon Rose, he did a series for Matrix, a local night spot. Moscoso's style is most notable for its visual intensity, which is obtained by manipulating form and color to create optical effects. Moscoso's use of contrasting colors and vibrating edges was influenced by painter Josef Albers, his teacher at Yale. Given Moscoso's sophistication, it is not surprising that he was the first of the rock poster artists to use photographic collage.

STANLEY MOUSE (born 1940)

Born in Detroit, Stanley "Mouse" Miller began his artistic career in the late 1950s, "pinstriping" cars and airbrushing designs on T-shirts while traveling around the country with the hot-rod circuit. During this period he was also a part-time student at the Art School of the Society of Arts and Crafts in Detroit. In 1963 he established his own corporation, Mouse Studios, producing a line of decals, posters, and T-shirts.

Mouse moved to Berkeley, California, in 1964, where he first met the artists associated with the Family Dog organization, which produced dance concerts at the Avalon Ballroom.

Mouse later replaced poster artist Wes Wilson at Family Dog and, beginning in June 1966, in collaboration with Alton Kelley, helped to establish the psychedelic style of expression under the name "Mouse Studios." This creative team produced a number of striking concert posters over the next two years, incorporating humor and commercial images that resonated in the hippie culture, with one of the most famous featuring ZigZag cigarette rolling papers.

When the demand for rock posters dropped off in the 1970s, Mouse and Kelley moved on to rock T-shirts and album covers. Their cover for Steve Miller's album, *Book of Dreams,* won a Grammy Award in 1977. Although production was limited, Mouse and Kelley's 1978 *Blue Rose* poster, created to commemorate the closing of the Winterland Arena, is considered a classic from this decade. Mouse currently lives with his wife in Sonoma, California. He has made a career licensing the commercial rights to his rock designs and is also working to establish his reputation as a fine art painter.

PATRICK NAGEL (1945–1984)

After completing his military service in Vietnam in the 1970s, Patrick Nagel began to attract an international audience for his images of sensual, mysterious women, which were reminiscent of Art Deco and Japanese woodblocks. He designed album covers, magazine illustrations, posters, and limited edition prints; he was also a painter and sculptor. Nagel built his reputation as one of *Playboy* magazine's most popular illustrators for almost a decade. He died at the age of thirty-eight after performing an aerobics routine at a charity benefit.

ALICE NEEL (1900–1984)

Born in Merion Square, Pennsylvania, Alice Neel graduated from the Philadelphia School of Design for Women (now Moore College of Art) in 1925. She was a portrait painter whose work cut across the social classes. She once described herself as a "collector of souls" and lived much of her adult life in the Spanish Harlem section of New York City. From 1935 to 1943, Neel was employed by the WPA Federal Art Project, Easel Division. In 1979 she was also included in a group exhibition of acclaimed women artists in Washington, D.C., entitled "Women's Caucus for Art Honors: Bishop, Burke, Neel, Nevelson, O'Keefe."

ERIK NITSCHE (born 1908)

Born in Lausanne, Switzerland, Erik Nitsche studied at the College Classique in Lausanne and then at the Kunstgewerbeschüle in Munich, Germany. In Paris he studied with Maximilien Vox and worked with the

Draeger Frères printing firm from 1929 to 1932. Moving to New York in 1934, he became art director for Saks Fifth Avenue, also working for Bloomingdale's, Macy's, and other stores. His wide range of clients includes The Museum of Modern Art, Decca Records, and General Dynamics Corporation's "Atoms for Peace" campaign. Since 1960, he has focused on book design.

GEORGIA O'KEEFFE (1887–1986)

Georgia O'Keeffe was born near Sun Prairie, Wisconsin, in 1887. During her teens and early adulthood, O'Keeffe lived in Virginia, Chicago, and New York. She studied with John Vanderpoel at the Art Institute of Chicago, with William Merritt Chase at the Art Students League in New York, and with Arthur Wesley Dow at Columbia University. O'Keeffe taught at Columbia College (South Carolina), at the University of Virginia, and at West Texas State Normal School. Her first important exhibition was in 1917 at 291 gallery, which was run by photographer Alfred Stieglitz, whom O'Keeffe would later marry. She lived and worked in New York beginning in 1918 and began spending summers in New Mexico in 1929. In 1949, O'Keeffe moved to New Mexico to live year-round.

O'Keeffe received a commission from Cheney Brothers, a silk company, but she later expressed reservations about commercial art, however; in 1924, O'Keeffe wrote to her sister Catherine: "You see I tried commercial Art. . . . I was a failure. . . . And I tried doing other foolish forms of commercial Art – I could make a living at it – but it wasn't worth the price. . . . Always thinking for a foolish idea for a foolish place didn't appeal to me for a steady diet – so I gambled on this foolish business of painting – and here I am at it."

O'Keeffe's husband and major promoter, Alfred Stieglitz, discouraged the reproduction of her works for fear that the paintings would be compromised. Nevertheless, O'Keeffe's art has frequently been used successfully on posters, most notably for the Santa Fe Chamber Music Festival. Since its first year in 1973, the festival has used a reproduction of an O'Keeffe painting, with her permission, and sold the poster nationally. O'Keeffe's art lends itself to posters, with the crisp lines, rich colors, and abstracted, simple shapes characteristic of her paintings.

TONY PALLADINO (born 1930)

The son of Italian immigrants, Tony Palladino was born in New York City and began his artistic training at the High School of Music and Art. In the late 1940s, he studied with Robert Motherwell, Mark Rothko, and William Baziotes in New York. In 1954, he began teaching graphic design at the School of Visual Arts. Palladino applies his boisterous creativity to both commercial and fine art. He was inducted into the New York Art Directors' Club Hall of Fame in 1987. In 1989, he transformed hubcaps into hats for a solo exhibition at the New York University's Broadway Windows gallery.

MAXFIELD PARRISH (1870–1966)

Maxfield Parrish was educated at the Pennsylvania Academy of the Fine Arts in his native city of Philadelphia. He also studied with the renowned illustrator Howard Pyle, who was an important influence on his work. Trained as both a painter and an illustrator, Parrish became one of the East Coast's preeminent poster designers in the 1890s. In 1896 his design was awarded first place from a pool of 525 entries in the competition for the Pope Bicycle poster, and from then on he was one of America's most frequently reproduced and prolific artists. Like so many of his contemporaries, Parrish designed posters for many book publishers. He was also successful in executing commercial commissions for such products as Colgate soap.

EDWARD PENFIELD (1866–1925)

Edward Penfield received his training at the Art Students League in New York City. He went on to become the art director at *Harper's* magazine and also designed a series of monthly posters for *Harper's* that won enormous critical acclaim. By the turn of the century, Penfield's reputation as an important graphic designer was assured.

The *Harper's* posters have been characterized as the definitive graphic works of the 1890s. Penfield took full advantage of recent improvements in color printing to create works that were effective vehicles of communication and also aesthetically engaging. Less concerned with the dramatic curving lines of Art Nouveau than his contemporary Will Bradley, Penfield synthesized a number of stylistic sources in his work, including Japanese prints and those of French artists such as Henri de Toulouse-Lautrec and Jules Chéret.

After leaving *Harper's* in 1901, Penfield continued to be extremely active in both design and illustration. In addition to posters for other magazines including *Scribner's* and *Collier's,* he executed illustrations and covers for many books and also generated designs for numerous commercial concerns. Together with Will Bradley, Penfield was instrumental in creating the rich fabric of American graphic design work in the 1890s.

JOSEPH PENNELL (1857–1926)
Born in Philadelphia, Pennell graduated from Germantown Friends school. He first studied art at the School of Industrial Art (now the Philadelphia College of Art), and later at the Pennsylvania Academy of Fine Arts. Both as a friend and biographer of James Abbott McNeill Whistler, Pennell worked as either a writer or illustrator on more than one hundred books. Pennell frequently collaborated on art and travel books with his wife, Elizabeth Robins Pennell.

For publications such as *Century, McClure's,* and *Harper's,* Pennell traveled the world, producing etchings, pen-and-ink drawings, and lithographs of cathedrals, plazas, street scenes, and palaces. He also made panoramic views of major construction and engineering projects, such as the Panama Canal and the locks at Niagara Falls. During World War I he created a number of important poster designs as a part of Charles Dana Gibson's Division of Pictorial Publicity of the Federal Committee of Public Information, which was organized when the United States entered the war in 1917. Pennell characterized the relationship of government to the arts at the time: "When the United States wished to make public its wants, whether of men or money, it found that art – as the European countries had found – was the best medium."

FREDERICK WINTHROP RAMSDELL (1865–1915)
Recognized as a landscape and portrait painter, Frederick Ramsdell studied in Paris and at the Art Students League in New York. After spending several years in Europe, Ramsdell returned to the United States and joined a colony of painters in Lyme, Connecticut.

PAUL RAND (1914–1997)
Paul Rand was one of the most influential graphic designers of the twentieth century. Born in New York City, Rand was educated at Pratt Institute, Parsons School of Design, and the Art Students League, where he worked with George Grosz. From 1936 to 1941 he served as the art editor for *Esquire* magazine, and he taught at the Advertising Guild, Pratt, Cooper Union, and Yale University, where he was professor emeritus of graphic design. He received awards from the American Institute of Graphic Arts and the Art Directors Club of New York and was given an honorary doctorate by the Philadelphia College of Art.

Rand designed the logos for a number of major commercial firms, including IBM, the American Broadcasting Company, and Westinghouse Corporation. His commitment to design education, combined with his writings and numerous visual innovations, constitute a lasting legacy for American designers.

Rand's poster designs reflected his theoretical writings on this art form. In one important essay he emphasized the need for a poster to work as a cohesive facet of the environment for which it is intended, and he discussed at length the different consequences that this interdependence can have on all aspects of the design process. The theme of integration and harmony in design was a constant for Rand. Writing in 1970 on the process of effective graphic design, he stated:

> *The designer does not, as a rule, begin with some preconceived idea. Rather the idea is . . . the result of careful study and observation, and the design is the product of that idea. In order, therefore, to achieve an effective solution to the problem the designer must necessarily go through some sort of mental process. Consciously or not, he analyzes, interprets, formulates. He is aware of the scientific and technological developments in his own and kindred fields. He improvises, invents, or discovers new techniques and combinations. He coordinates and integrates his material so that he may restate his problem in terms of ideas, signs, symbols, pictures. He unifies, simplifies, and eliminates superfluities. He symbolizes – abstracts from his material by association and analogy. . . . He draws upon instinct and intuition. He considers the spectator, his feelings and predilections.*

ROBERT RAUSCHENBERG (born 1925)
Trained at the Kansas City Art Institute and at the Art

Students League in New York, Robert Rauschenberg introduced his first "mixed-media" paintings in 1955 after working with Willem de Kooning. The combination of painted images with found objects was part of the artist's effort to break down the boundaries between art and life. Extending this idea, Rauschenberg collaborated with composer John Cage and dancer Merce Cunningham on a series of performances later labeled as "happenings." Rauschenberg's early work is distinguished by the juxtaposition of disparate images using photo-transfer and silkscreen in combination with painted forms and found objects. His experimental methods are credited with opening the door for the Pop art movement.

ETHEL REED (born 1874)

In the last decade of the nineteenth century, Ethel Reed emerged as one of Boston's preeminent poster designers. Born in Newburyport, Massachusetts, she studied drawing and was briefly apprenticed to a painter of miniatures, but for the most part was self-taught. She spent most of her brief career in Boston and also did some work in London.

Reed was extraordinarily prolific while in Boston. From 1895 to 1897 she designed a large number of important book posters, in addition to producing illustrations, covers, and endpapers for many books. Her style was distinctive, albeit rooted in the sensibility of Art Nouveau. Many of Reed's illustrations feature female figures, frequently surrounded by objects and tangled forms that seem full of secret and illicit meanings.

Reed's departure from the spotlight was even more sudden than her arrival. Engaged to the Boston artist Philip Hale in 1897, she traveled to England later that year to work on a book poster for the novelist Richard Le Gallienne. She then traveled to Ireland, apparently for a vacation. At this point she disappeared, and nothing more is known of her activities or whereabouts.

FELICE REGAN (born 1948)

Felice Regan has had a long love affair with art and nature, which began in 1970 when she started producing photographic silkscreen images of animals at the Franklin Park Zoo outside of Boston. That same year, Regan received her B.F.A. degree from the Massachusetts College of Art and promptly founded the Graphic Workshop, an artists' collaborative.

At the outset, the workshop offered few paid jobs. Money, however, was never a driving factor. According to Kevin McCollough, a Harvard business student, "the workshop was really subsidized with sweat, blood, friendship, and everybody living cheap." As long as Regan and her friends had a place and the materials to express their artistic ideas, they and the workshop would survive.

In 1975, they got their first big break designing posters for the World Society for the Protection of Animals. Even after the project fell through, Regan decided to proceed anyway, creating what became known as the "Endangered Species" series. The series, which has become a trademark of the workshop, led Regan and her colleagues to produce some of their best-known works.

Today, the Graphic Workshop is a viable commercial enterprise, providing both the space and the freedom for imaginative work. Felice Regan continues to encourage new generations of poster artists as a guest lecturer at the Massachusetts College of Art.

LOUIS JOHN RHEAD (1857–1926)

Born in Staffordshire, England, Louis John Rhead studied at the National Art Training School in London and in Paris with Gustave-Rodolphe-Clarence Boulanger. In 1883, he moved to New York, where he worked as art director for the publisher D. Appleton for six years. Rhead also designed patterns for ceramic painting and art needlework for women's magazines, as well as designing book covers and painting. From 1891 to 1894 he continued his studies in London and Paris, influenced by the Swiss-French artist Eugène Grasset's style, which infused his posters with moral content. Rhead was also influenced by Walter Crane and William Morris, two English artists involved with the Aesthetic movement.

In the 1890s Rhead designed nearly one hundred posters. His first posters were done in England for *Cassell's Magazine*, the *Weekly Dispatch*, and also for Phitesi boots. In the United States he created posters for a variety of magazines, including *The Century, St. Nicholas, Harper's, The Bookman,* and *Scribner's.* He also produced large, one- and two-sheet posters for the *New York Sun* and the *New York Journal*, and commercial posters for the printing firm Louis Prang and Company, as well as for products such as Lundborg perfumes, Pearline washing powders, and Packer's soap.

Rhead's posters were widely acclaimed; solo exhibitions of his work were presented in London in 1896, and in Paris at the Salon des Cent in 1897. After 1900, Rhead created illustrations for literary works and wrote several books on fishing.

LARRY RIVERS (born 1925)
Born Larry Grossberg in the Bronx, New York, Rivers started his career as a jazz saxophonist in 1940. While studying at The Juilliard School in 1944, a fellow student introduced Rivers to the work of Georges Braque, which sparked in him an interest in painting. In 1948, he enrolled in the art education program at New York University and received his degree in 1951.

Rivers is a versatile artist who has worked in a wide range of media. Recognized for his interest in historical images and themes, he has also produced a number of collaborative works with other artists, including poets Frank O'Hara and Kenneth Koch and sculptor Jean Tinguely. Additionally, Rivers has designed stage sets for Stravinsky's *Oedipus Rex* and for two of LeRoi Jones's plays, and worked with Pierre Gaisseau on the television documentary "Africa and I."

NORMAN ROCKWELL (1894–1978)
Norman Rockwell was born in New York City, where he began his art training in 1908 at the Chase School of Fine and Applied Art – taking classes there in addition to his regular high school studies. In 1910 he quit high school to study art full-time at the National Academy School, but later that same year transferred to the Art Students League. Rockwell's career advanced rapidly; at nineteen he became art director of *Boy's Life*, and at twenty-two he painted a cover for the *Saturday Evening Post* – the first of 324 covers he created for that magazine. Rockwell's posters, while not as numerous as his magazine illustrations, were done for a wide variety of organizations and issues. Early in his career, in the 1920s and 1930s, he made posters for products such as Coca-Cola and Maxwell House coffee. His movie posters include those for *Along Came Jones* (1945), *The Razor's Edge* (1946), and *Stagecoach* (1966). He also created posters for *Parents'* magazine

and *McCall's*, as well as for the Red Cross and the National Reserve.

Rockwell received many honors, including the 1969 Artist of the Year award from the Artists' Guild of New York and the Freedom Award from President Gerald Ford. A museum devoted to his work, the Norman Rockwell Museum, was established in Philadelphia in 1976. The Norman Rockwell Museum in Stockbridge, Massachusetts, opened in 1993 and now holds the world's largest collection of original Rockwell art.

RAYMOND JENNINGS SAUNDERS (born 1934)
Born in Pittsburgh, Pennsylvania, Raymond Saunders earned a B.F.A. degree from the Carnegie Institute of Technology. He later studied at the Pennsylvania Academy of Fine Arts, the University of Pennsylvania, and eventually received an M.F.A. from California College of Arts and Crafts in 1961. Saunders works in many media, including watercolor, painting, drawing, collage, and assemblage. His familiarity with many media often produces gestural, painterly collages with origins in the loose brushstrokes and large color fields of the Abstract Expressionists; his works are also indebted to the playfulness of Pop art. Saunders's work has been collected by many prominent institutions such as New York's Metropolitan Museum of Art, The Museum of Modern Art, and the Whitney Museum of American Art. Saunders currently lives and works in California.

BEN SHAHN (1898–1969)
Born in Lithuania, Ben Shahn immigrated to the United States in 1906. In his early teens he worked as a lithographer's apprentice, but he went on to study biology at New York University. Shahn later changed course, studying at the Art Students League and, in 1925, at the Académie de la Grande Chaumière in Paris. Returning to the United States in 1929, he worked as a photographer for the Farm Security Administration from 1935 to 1938. Over the years, Shahn experimented with silkscreening and created magazine illustrations and advertisements.

During his lithography apprenticeship Shahn grew to appreciate the relationships of lettering. "I enjoyed a year or so of complete infatuation with type," he stated. "I set everything that I could in types with which I was beginning to be familiar; I did posters all in type – a strange turn for an artist – or posters in which type boldly predominated." Shahn designed posters for the Office of War Information in 1942 and for other government departments from 1944 to 1946.

Shahn was a teacher and lecturer at many institutions, ranging from the Universities of Colorado and Wisconsin to Black Mountain College and Harvard University. Named one of the ten best American painters by *Look* magazine in 1948, he had many solo exhibitions during his career.

DAVID SINGER (born 1941)

David Singer grew up in Pennsylvania Dutch country, where he was exposed to antiques and folk art. Another influence on his work, perhaps related to the hex signs of folk art, was his childhood interest in geometric forms. Although Singer had little formal art training, his polished presentation and prodigious output made him one of the most respected poster artists emerging in the late 1960s in San Francisco.

Not initially interested in making posters, Singer assembled a portfolio of collages that he envisioned as "greeting cards or something." His work was rejected by most of the publishers in San Francisco before gaining immediate acceptance from Bill Graham, a dance-concert promoter for the Fillmore Auditorium. During the Fillmore era, from 1969 to 1971, Singer created more posters for Graham than any other artist, most notably the double-size final poster evoking the Fillmore experience. Even after the Fillmore closed in 1971, Singer continued to create posters commemorating special events sponsored by Graham. To a great extent, Singer was a transitional rock-poster artist; his works possessed a refinement, even a polish that would dominate the 1970s rock world. During that decade he produced significant posters for the Rolling Stones, the Who, and Santana.

Singer's posters are notable for his use of collage, incorporating thousands of images clipped from magazines spanning several decades. He developed a format that included a stunning variety of lettering styles, applying them in close relation to the theme or subject of a poster.

JOHN SLOAN (1871–1951)

Educated at the Pennsylvania Academy of the Fine Arts, John Sloan began his career in the visual arts as an illustrator for the *Philadelphia Inquirer* and went on to become one of America's best-known painters and printmakers.

Sloan was an important member of the Ashcan School, a group of painters working in New York City during the first decades of the twentieth century. Sloan's painting is marked by a characteristic crowding of forms and grainy tonality that sought to convey the rapid movement and changing atmosphere of the new metropolis.

Sloan was also an accomplished illustrator and graphic designer. His drawings were published in periodicals such as *Everybody's Magazine, Harper's Weekly, Collier's,* and *The Chap-Book.* Participating in the enthusiasm for posters that swept the country in the 1890s, Sloan designed his first poster in 1893. He went on to produce posters for numerous commercial firms and also for *Moods, The Echo,* and the publisher Copeland and Day. A number of his designs reveal the influence of Japanese prints, an interest he shared with many of his fellow artists. Sloan spoke in particular of having been influenced by the Japanese artist Beizen Zubota. He was also aware of the impact of English artist Aubrey Beardsley's work on many American poster designers. However, Sloan was not entirely comfortable with Beardsley's work, as he noted in a discussion of the artists who had influenced him:

> *My poster style was always different from Beardsley's. It was done from memory and imagination of real life and is less ornamental in design. While I admire some of Beardsley's remarkable patterns and skillful drawing, I myself do not care for the kind of decadent and bizarre quality in his work. I prefer the wholesome kind of humor that comes out in ribaldry. Of the French poster artists I was most influenced by Steinlen. I liked the humanism with which he drew people, and learned from him technical devices about using crayon to make shading which could be used for linecut reproduction. It was mostly from a study of Japanese prints that I found fresh ideas about design, discovered in observing everyday life.*

JOHN HENRY TWACHTMAN (1853–1902)

Born in Cincinnati, John Henry Twachtman gained an early exposure to art, observing his father paint fruit, flowers, and landscapes on shades at Breneman Brothers window-shade factory. In his teens Twachtman also began to work at the factory. He enrolled in night classes in drawing at the Ohio Mechanics Institute and then attended the McMicken School. Twachtman's European training included two years at the Royal Academy in Munich and three years at the Académie Julian in Paris. Settling in Greenwich, Connecticut, in 1889, he produced many of the Impressionist landscapes for which he is best known.

Twachtman's only known poster design was commissioned in 1896 by Stone & Kimball, promoting Harold Frederic's book *The Damnation of Theron Ware.* Revealing Twachtman's background as a painter, the design relies on subtle colors and brushwork more than the bold color contrasts and lines favored by postermakers of that era.

TOMI UNGERER (born 1931)

A native of Strasbourg, France, Ungerer has lived and worked in a number of places in Europe and North America. After spending World War II in Nazi-occupied Alsace, he briefly attended the École des Arts Décoratifs. Ungerer has stated that living under Nazi rule, combined with the death of his father when he was three, account for the dark nature of much of his work. From 1956 to the late 1960s he lived in New York; since then, he has resided in Nova Scotia, Strasbourg, and Ireland, among other places.

Ungerer's versatility has earned him enormous fame during the last quarter century. In addition to extensive advertising work for a number of commercial firms in Europe and America, he has written and illustrated scores of books for adults and children, such as *The Three Robbers,* and has executed paintings and sculptures and worked in television and publishing. The recipient of numerous graphic design awards, Ungerer has exhibited his work on three continents, including a 1981 retrospective at the Musée des Arts Décoratifs in Paris.

Ungerer has been linked to the tradition of earlier social commentators in the visual arts. His dark, biting, often bleakly humorous satire has drawn inevitable comparisons with William Hogarth, Honoré Daumier, and George Grosz. Although his range of influences is broad, from Albrecht Dürer to Japanese artists such as Katsushika Hokusai, Ungerer has referred to himself as a "street artist," recording the complexity and degradation of modern society in an unmistakable, spare, yet insistently biting drawing style.

XAVIER VIRAMONTES (born 1943)

Xavier Viramontes was born in Richmond, California, and received a B.F.A. degree from San Francisco Art Institute and an M.A. from San Francisco State University. He was one of several artists and community activists who helped establish the *Galeria de la Raza* in San Francisco in order to exhibit works by Chicano and Mexican artists. As part of the *Galeria*'s educational outreach program he painted several temporary, billboard-sized murals on topics related to community goals. The poster *Boycott Grapes* was commissioned by the *Galeria de la Raza*'s founding director, Rene Yañez, to help support the work of the United Farm Worker's Union. Viramontes printed about twenty-five serigraphic impressions of the image and then gave the color separations to the UFW for offset lithography. When asked about political posters as an artistic medium, Viramontes wrote: "For making political statements, one can never underestimate the powers of a poster. A strong, well-executed image with few chosen words can make a great impact and can outlive the memories of past rallies or political marches."

The recipient of numerous printmaking awards, Viramontes has taught classes in etching, monoprint, linocut, and silkscreen techniques at City College in San Francisco since 1980. He is the chairman of the Fort Mason Campus Gallery which showcases City College student work.

WES WILSON (born 1937)

Wes Wilson attended San Francisco State University and was working at Contact Printing, a small San Francisco press, when his career as a psychedelic-poster artist took off. At Contact, Wilson did the layout and design for handbills that eventually established him as a poster designer. When the Avalon Ballroon and Bill Graham's Fillmore Auditorium began to hold weekly dance concerts, Wilson was called upon to design the posters. He created psychedelic posters from February 1966 until May 1967, when disputes over money severed his connection with Graham. Wilson's early work was unique, but by mid-1967 so many artists had copied his style that he was easily replaced.

Wilson claims that he was the first artist to create a psychedelic poster. Intended for a particular audience – one that was tuned in to the psychedelic experience – his art, especially the lugubrious, freehand lettering, emerged from Wilson's own involvement with that experience and the psychedelic art of light shows. His influential lettering was derived from the Vienna Secessionist lettering he discovered in a University of California exhibition catalogue.

Wilson's approach to postermaking was quite improvisatory. According to the artist, he selected colors through visual experiences with LSD, as well as from his professional experience as a printer. Eventually disillusioned with the career and financial opportunities of poster art, he moved to the Missouri Ozarks, where he lives on a farm.

THE WPA/FAP POSTER DIVISION
Written by Leo Costello

A number of postermakers included in this book worked for the Poster Division of the WPA's Federal Art Project, including Albert M. Bender, Carken, and Jack Rivolta. The history of this project can be traced to October 24, 1929, when the stock-market crash signaled the beginning of the Great Depression, an era of economic hardship that would last until the United States entered World War II. By 1933, unemployment had reached 25 percent, and many artists, like other people throughout the country, had no means of support.

With his inauguration in 1933, President Franklin Delano Roosevelt fulfilled a campaign promise to launch massive social relief programs. Roosevelt's New Deal included programs unprecedented in scale that sought to provide members of all levels of society with a living wage for public work. These efforts also aimed to raise the country's overall standard of living. Despite the opposition of conservative critics and politicians, the programs went forward. Established in May 1935, the Works Progress Administration (WPA), later known as the Works Projects Administration, employed approximately 2.1 million Americans in public works programs ranging from surveying and construction to agricultural engineering and art making.

The largest of the New Deal programs for unemployed artists was the Federal Art Project (FAP). Produced under its auspices was an extraordinarily large volume of work that ran the gamut from easel paintings and murals to sculpture and various graphic arts. The FAP was also committed to making the arts accessible to the general public. It sponsored art exhibitions nationwide and funded art education classes for adults and children in many American communities, establishing more than one hundred community art centers. Approximately one-third of the total number of artists working for the FAP were in New York City,[1] and it was here that the poster division was created in 1935.

This division began relatively slowly, with a small staff turning out a modest number of hand-lettered and hand-painted posters. By 1938, however, production had significantly increased due to the adoption of the far more efficient silkscreening method. Anthony Velonis, an experienced commercial designer in New York, brought the process to the FAP and described it in the following manner:

> A piece of gauze-like silk or organdy [is] stretched on a wooden frame. A thin delicate stencil [is] held by the web of the silk. Paint is "squeegeed" and the paint flows only through the part of the silk that is not obstructed by the stencil, depositing itself on the paper underneath. The first color is printed. It is permitted to dry. The next color is "squeegeed" through another stencil, and then the next, until the print is finished.[2]

The artists of the poster division produced some two million silkscreens based on roughly thirty-five thousand designs. They were responsible for creating designs for a wide range of governmental commissions, which were often used in public campaigns of other departments. Issues addressed by FAP postermakers included safety in the workplace, improved public health and housing, and education. They also frequently advertised FAP events, including exhibitions and Federal Theater Project productions. Although the New York office remained the largest, by 1938 branches of the poster division were operating in eighteen states.[3]

With the exception of a few key artists, relatively little biographical information is available about many of those who worked in the FAP poster division, owing in part, to the fact that many posters were created collaboratively, and artists were not allowed to sign their work.[4] This reflects a governmental approach to the arts that differed from the traditional view, which values individual expression and accomplishment. The initial goals of the Federal Art Project were avowedly social rather than artistic. "Its primary concern was with the artist – not with art as such," said Holger Cahill, national director of the Art Project in 1938.[5] Because of its explicitly social content and governmental sponsorship, past art-historical scholarship has generally excluded the work done for the FAP from the realm of "high art." Recently, however, these works have been recognized as valuable not only as cultural documents but also as aesthetically powerful and formally innovative images.

Many of the best WPA posters certainly meet both of these criteria. Administrators such as Richard Floethe fostered an environment of adventurous creativity that gave rise to groundbreaking designs. In many ways, the FAP poster artists were at the forefront of incorporating progressive design strategies culled from a variety of international sources, such as the Russian Constructivists's creative use of typeface. A product of the famed Bauhaus design school in Germany, Floethe brought many of its innovations to the poster division.[6] It has been further suggested that the sense of relative artistic liberty nurtured by Floethe and others was reinforced by the fact that the artists were working for government clients and therefore not constrained by the need to sell products that governs commercial design.[7]

Conservative opposition to the WPA and the FAP eventually succeeded in forcing cutbacks in funding and placing restrictions on their scope and independence. Colonel Brehon Somervell, a career military officer and head of the New York WPA projects, alienated many artists in the FAP with his pragmatic and, in their view, arbitrary and heavy-handed artistic standards. In 1938 and 1939 reductions in FAP staff and offices were mandated in many divisions, including poster design. Activities did continue, although on a significantly reduced scale, until 1942 when the poster division was placed under the auspices of the Defense Department and its efforts shifted to projects related to the war effort.

The Federal Art Project holds an important place in the history of American art. The work it produced raised public awareness about numerous issues, made important design innovations, and, perhaps most significantly,

allowed an enormous number of artists, including Lee Krasner, Stuart Davis, Jackson Pollock, and Will Barnet, to earn a living in their profession during hard times. The work of the division has provided a continuing legacy of American graphic design and creativity. Its accomplishments were effectively characterized by designer Jim Heimann:

> *Taken as an aggregate, the posters display a skilled application and synthesis of modern fine art and commercial art principles of the first four decades of the twentieth century. In addition to providing public service, the posters exposed the public to sophisticated art applied to the commonplace.*[8]

NOTES

1. Christopher DeNoon, ed., *Posters of the WPA* (Los Angeles: Wheatley Press/University of Washington Press, 1987): 17.
2. Francis O'Connor, comp., *Art for the Millions: Essays by Artists and Administrators of the WPA Federal Art Project* (Greenwich, Conn.: New York Graphic Society, 1979): 156.
3. DeNoon, 22.
4. DeNoon, 129.
5. Gerald E. Markowitz and Marlene Park, *New Deal for Art: The Government Art Projects from the 1930s with Examples from New York City and State* (Hamilton, N.Y.: Gallery Association of New York, 1977): 7.
6. Jeannie Friedman, "WPA Poster Project: When Government Sponsors Art," *Print* (July/Aug. 1978).
7. DeNoon, 24.
8. DeNoon, 111.

Bibliography

Compiled by Julie Charles

Ades, Dawn. *The 20th-Century Poster: Design of the Avant-Garde*. Exh. cat. Minneapolis: Walker Art Center; New York: Abbeville Press, Inc., 1984.

Alexandre, Arsene. *The Modern Poster*. New York: Charles Scribner's Sons, 1895.

Allner, W. H. *Posters*. New York: Reinhold, 1952.

Allyn, Nancy E. H. *Broadsides & Posters from the National Archives*. Washington, D.C.: National Archives and Record Service, 1986.

Art and Commerce: American Prints of the Nineteenth Century. Charlottesville: University Press of Virginia, 1978.

Banta, Martha. *Imaging American Women: Idea and Ideals in Cultural History*. New York: Columbia University Press, 1987.

Barnicoat, John. *A Concise History of Posters*. New York: Harry N. Abrams, Inc., 1972, 1988.

Bayer, Herbert. *Herbert Bayer: Painter, Designer, Architect*. New York: Reinhold, 1967.

Belsito, Peter, Bob Davis, and Marian Kester. *STREETART: The Punk Poster in San Francisco*. San Francisco: Last Gasp, 1981.

"Bill Graham Presents in San Francisco: A Poster Checklist." San Francisco: Winterland Productions, c. 1978.

Bird, Elisha Brown. *Poster Lore* 1 (April 1896).

Black, Lisa, and Victor Zurbel, eds. *Peter Max: A Retrospective, The Eastern European Museum Tour*. Los Angeles: Hanson Galleries, 1991.

Bradley, William H. *William Bradley: His Chap-Book*. New York: The Typophiles, 1955.

Brandt, Frederick R. *Designed to Sell: The Turn-of-the-Century American Posters*. Exh. cat. Richmond: Virginia Museum of Fine Arts, 1994.

Bredhoff, Stacey. *Powers of Persuasion: Poster Art from World War II*. Washington, D.C.: National Archives Office of Public Programs, 1994.

Breitenbach, Edgar. "The Poster Craze," *The American Heritage* 13, no. 2 (1962).

Breitenbach, Edgar, and Margaret Cogswell. *The American Poster*. Exh. cat. New York: American Federation of Arts/October House, 1967.

Brunner, Felix. *A Handbook of Graphic Reproduction Processes*. New York: Hastings House, 1984.

Catalogue of an Exhibition of Illustrated Bill-Posters. Exh. cat. New York: Grolier Club, 1890.

Chenault, Libby. *Battlelines: World War I Posters from the Bowman Gray Collection*. Chapel Hill and London: University of North Carolina Press, 1988.

Christy, Howard Chandler. *The American Girl*. New York: Moffatt, Yard and Company, 1906.

Cirker, Hayward, and Blanche Cirker. *The Golden Age of the Poster*. New York: Dover Publications, Inc., 1971.

Clark, Kenneth. *The Best of Aubrey Beardsley*. New York: Doubleday, Inc., 1978.

Cohen, Allen, ed. *San Francisco Oracle*. Oakland: Regent Press, 1991.

Collins, Tom. "Wes Wilson: Rock and Roll Posters as Art," *Daily Californian*, 30 Nov. 1966.

Connolly, L. *Posters and American War Posters, Historical and Explanatory*. Newark, N.J., 1917.

Conway, Robert. *Rockwell Kent: Prints and Drawings 1904–1962*. New York: Associated American Artists, 1987.

Corlett, Mary Lee. *The Prints of Roy Lichtenstein: A Catalogue Raisonné 1948–1993*. Introduction by Ruth E. Fine. New York: Hudson Hills Press, 1994.

Cullinane, Robert. *The Complete Book of Compre-hensives*. New York: Van Nostrand Reinhold, 1990.

Darracott, Joseph. *The First World War in Posters*. New York: Dover Publications, Inc., 1974.

Darracott, Joseph, and Belinda Loftus. *First World War Posters*. London: Imperial War Museum, 1972.

Davis, Paul, and Bernard Gersten. *Paul Davis: Posters and Paintings*. New York: E. P. Dutton, 1977.

Dembo, George M. "The Statue of Liberty in Posters: Creation of an American Icon," *P.S.: Quarterly Journal of the Poster Society* (Winter 1986–87): 18–21.

DeNoon, Christopher. *Posters of the WPA*. Los Angeles: Wheatley Press, 1987.

Downey, Fairfax. *Portrait of an Era as Drawn by C. D. Gibson*. New York: Charles Scribner's Sons, 1936.

Durant, John, and Alice Durant. *Pictorial History of the American Circus*. New York: A. S. Barnes, 1957.

Early American Theatrical Posters. Philadelphia: Ledger Job Printing Office, 1869–72.

Elzea, Rowland, and Betty Elzea. *The Pre-Raphaelite Era 1848–1914*. Exh. cat. Wilmington: Delaware Art Museum, 1976.

Falk, Peter Hastings, ed. *Who Was Who in American Art*. Madison, Conn.: Sound View Press, 1985.

Farren, Mick, ed. *Get on Down: A Decade of Rock & Roll Posters*. London: Big O Publishing, 1976.

Fern, Alan. *Word and Image*. New York: Museum of Modern Art, 1968.

———. *Lance Hidy's Posters: Designs Personal & Public*. Natick, Mass.: Alphabet Press, 1983.

———. *Off the Wall: Research into the Art of the Poster*. Chapel Hill, N.C.: Hanes Foundation, 1985.

Fern, Alan, and Mildred Constantine. *Revolutionary Soviet Film Posters*. Baltimore and London: Johns Hopkins University Press, 1974.

Fox, Charles Philip. *American Circus Posters in Full Color*. New York: Dover Publications, Inc., 1978.

Fox, Charles Philip, and Tom Parkinson. *Billers, Banners and Bombast: The Story of Circus Advertising*. Boulder, Colo.: Pruett, 1985.

Friedman, Ben. "A Guide to the Numbered Family Dog Posters." San Francisco: The Postermat, c. 1970.

Freidman, Jeannie. "WPA Poster Project: When Government Sponsors Art," *Print* (July/Aug. 1978).

Friedman, Mildred, and Phil Freshman, ed. *Graphic Design in America: A Visual Language History*. Exh. cat. Minneapolis: Walker Art Center, 1989.

Fullington, Greg. "The Poster Art of David Goines," *California Living*, 15 Mar. 1981.

Gallatin, Albert Eugene. *Art and the Great War*. New York: E. P. Dutton, 1919.

Gallo, Max. *The Poster in History*. New York: McGraw-Hill, 1974.

Gardner, Colin. "The Space between Words: Lawrence Weiner," *Artforum* (Nov. 1990).

Gibson, David. *Designed to Persuade: Graphic Art of Edward Penfield*. Exh. cat. Yonkers, N.Y.: The Hudson River Museum, 1984.

Glueck, Grace. "Alice Neel, Self-Styled 'Collector of Souls,' Unfurls Her Own, in Glee and Heartbreak." *New York Times,* 21 Mar. 1997.

Goddu, Joseph. *Posters of the 1890s*. New York: Hirschl & Adler Galleries, 1989.

Goines, David Lance. *David Lance Goines Posters: 1970–1994*. Berkeley, Calif.: Ten Speed Press Logo, 1971.

———. *David Lance Goines Posters*. Natick, Mass.: Alphabet Press, 1985.

Goldman, David. "Doing the Convention Rock: Griffin and Kelley at the Rock Ages Convention," *Relix* 8, no. 3 (June 1981).

Goldman, Shifra. "A Public Voice: Fifteen Years of Chicano Posters," *Art Journal* (spring 1984): 50–57.

"Graphics: Nouveau Frisco," *Time*, 7 April 1967.

"The Great Poster Wave: Expendable Graphic Art Becomes America's Biggest Hang-Up," *Life*, 1 Sept. 1967.

Great Propaganda Posters: Paper Bullets, Axis and Allied Countries WW II. New York and London: Chelsea House Publishers, 1977.

Green, Blake. "Poster Pals Gather Again: Artists of the '60s Relive their Psychedelic Successes," *San Francisco Chronicle*, 1 Oct. 1985.

Griffin, Rick, and Gordon McClelland. *Rick Griffin*. New York: Perige Books, 1980.

Grushkin, Paul D. *The Art of Rock. Posters from Presley to Punk*. New York: Abbeville Press, Inc., 1987.

Guerrilla Girls. *Confessions of the Guerrilla Girls*. New York: Harper Perennial, 1995.

Hagerty, Donald I. *Desert Dreams: The Art and Life of Maynard Dixon*. New York: Gibbs-Smith Publisher, 1993.

Harper, Paula. *War, Revolution & Peace: Propaganda Posters from the Hoover Institution Archives 1914–1945*. Exh. cat. Stanford, Calif.: Hoover Institution Press, 1969.

Hawkes, Elizabeth H. *The Poster Decade: American Posters of the 1890s*. Exh. cat. Wilmington: Delaware Art Museum, 1977.

Heller, Steven. *Graphic Design in America*. Minneapolis: Walker Art Center/Harry N. Abrams, Inc., 1989.

———. "Experimental Typography: Victor Moscoso, Master of Psychedelic Lettering," *U & lc* 47 (fall 1990): 26–29.

Heller, Steven, and Seymour Chwast. "Design and Style (No. 1): Jugendstil." New York: Mohawk Paper Mills/The Push Pin Group, 1986.

Hiatt, Charles. *Picture Posters*. London: George Bell and Sons, 1895.

Higbee, William Tryon. *Some Posters*. Cleveland: Imperial Press, 1895.

Hillier, Bevis. *Posters*. New York: Stein and Day, 1969.

———. *100 Years of Posters*. London: Pall Mall Press, 1972.

Horn, Maurice, ed. *Contemporary Graphic Artists*. Detroit: Gale Research Company, 1988.

Hornung, Clarence P., ed. *Will Bradley: His Graphic Art*. New York: Dover Publications, Inc., 1974.

Hutchinson, Harold. *The Poster: An Illustrated History*. New York: Viking Press, 1968.

Hyman, Helen S. *Designed To Persuade: American Literary Advertising Posters of the 1890s*. Exh. cat. New Haven: Yale University Art Gallery, 1978.

Images of an Era: The American Poster 1945–75. Introduction by John Garrigan. Washington, D.C.: National Collection of Fine Arts, Smithsonian Institution, 1975.

Jackson, Blair, and Regan McMahon. "Art for Fun's Sake: The Magical World of Alton Kelley," *The Golden Road* (summer 1984).

Jacobs, Karrie, and Steven Heller. *Angry Graphics: Protest Posters of the Reagan/Bush Era*. Salt Lake City: Peregrine Smith Books, 1992.

James Montgomery Flagg. Exh. cat. New York: Berry-Hill Galleries, 1971.

Johnson, J. Stewart. *The Modern American Poster from the Graphic Design Collection of The Museum of Modern Art New York*. Exh. cat. New York: Museum of Modern Art, 1984.

Kauffer, E. McKnight. *The Art of the Poster*. London: Cecil Palmer, 1924.

Keay, Carolyn. *American Posters of the Turn of the Century*. New York: St. Martin's Press, 1975.

Keen, Sam. *Faces of the Enemy: Reflections of the Hostile Imagination*. New York: Harper & Row, 1986.

———. *Voices and Visions*. New York: Harper & Row, 1974.

Kernan, Michael. "Gee!! It's Christy," *Washington Post*, 11 Jan. 1980.

Kiehl, David W. *American Art Posters of the 1890s in The Metropolitan Museum of Art, Including the Leonard A. Lauder Collection*. New York: Metropolitan Museum of Art, 1987.

King, Eric. *A Collector's Guide to the Numbered Dance Posters Created for Bill Graham and the Family Dog: 1966–1973*. Berkeley, Calif.: Svaha Press, 1980.

Kisch, John, and Edward Mapp. *A Separate Cinema: Fifty Years of Black-Cast Posters*. New York: Farrar, Straus & Giroux, 1992.

Kloster, Donald E., and Edward C. Ezell. "American Posters and the First World War." *AB Bookman's Weekly* 79 (29 June 1987): 2879–84.

Kobal, John. *Fifty Years of Movie Posters*. London: Hamlyn, 1973.

Kozik, Frank. *Man's Ruin: The Posters and Art of Frank Kozik*. San Francisco: Last Gasp, 1995.

———. Interview by Therese Heyman, tape recording, San Francisco, 24 Oct. 1996.

Krantz, Les. *American Artists*. New York: Krantz Company Publishers, 1985.

Kunzle, David. *Art as a Political Weapon: American Posters of Protest 1966–70*. New York: New School Art Center, 1971.

———. *Posters of Protest: The Posters of Political Satire in the U.S. 1966–1970*. Goleta, Calif.: University of California, Santa Barbara, 1971.

LaLiberte, Norman. *The Book of Posters*. Blauvelt, N.Y.: Art Education, 1970.

Larry Rivers: From the Coloring Book of Japan. New York: Marlborough Gallery, Inc., 1974.

Lederer, Carrie. *Guerrilla Girls Talk Back: The First Five Years. A Retrospective: 1985–1990.* Exh. cat. San Rafael, Calif.: Falkirk Cultural Center, 1991.

Lehrer, Ruth Fine. "J. J. Gould, Jr." In *Philadelphia: Three Centuries of American Art.* Exh. cat. Philadelphia: Philadelphia Museum of Art, 1976.

———. "Joseph Pennell." In *Philadelphia: Three Centuries of American Art.* Exh. cat. Philadelphia: Philadelphia Museum of Art, 1976.

Lippard, Lucy R. *Rupert García : Prints and Posters 1967–1990.* Exh. cat. San Francisco: Fine Arts Museums of San Francisco, 1991.

List, Vera, and Herbert Kupferberg. *Lincoln Center Posters.* New York: Harry N. Abrams, Inc., 1980.

Livingstone, Alan, and Isabella Livingstone. *The Thames and Hudson Encyclopedia of Graphic Design and Designers.* London: Thames and Hudson, 1992.

Ludwig, Coy. *Maxfield Parrish.* New York: Watson-Guptill, 1973.

Lupton, Ellen. *Mixing Messages.* New York: Cooper-Hewitt National Design Museum, Smithsonian Institution; Princeton, N.J.: Princeton Architectural Press, 1996.

Magnus, Gunter Hugo. *Graphic Techniques for Designers and Illustrators.* Woodbury, N.Y. and Toronto: Barron's, 1980.

Margolin, Victor. *American Poster Renaissance. The Great Age of Poster Design 1890–1900.* New York: Watson-Guptill, 1975.

———. *The Golden Age of the American Poster.* New York: Ballantine, 1976.

Markowitz, Gerald E., and Marlene Park. *New Deal for Art: The Government Art Projects from the 1930s with Examples from New York City and State.* Hamilton, N. Y.: Gallery Association of New York, 1977.

Max, Peter. *The Peter Max Poster Book.* New York: Crown, 1970.

McDonald, William F. *Federal Relief Administration and the Arts.* Columbus: Ohio State University, 1969.

McKinnon, Liliclaire C. "Biographical Text." In *Norman Rockwell: The Great American Storyteller.* Jackson: Mississippi Museum of Art, 1989.

McQuiston, Liz. *Graphic Agitation: Social and Political Graphics Since the Sixties.* London: Phaidon Press, 1993.

Medieros, Walter. "San Francisco Rock Concert Posters: Imagery and Meaning" (master's thesis, University of California, Berkeley, 1972).

———. *San Francisco Rock Poster Art.* Preface by Henry Hopkins. Exh. cat. San Francisco: San Francisco Museum of Modern Art, 1976.

Metropolitan Museum of Art Bulletin 34, no. 1 (spring 1976).

Metzl, Ervine. *The Poster: Its History and Its Art.* New York: Watson-Guptill, 1963.

Meyer, Susan E. *James Montgomery Flagg.* New York: Watson-Guptill, 1974.

———. *America's Great Illustrators.* New York: Harry N. Abrams, Inc., 1978.

Millie, Elena G. "College Poster Art." *Art Journal* 44 (spring 1984): 58–61.

Mills, Vernon. *Making Posters.* New York: Watson-Guptill, 1967.

Minkler, Doug. "Proselytizing From the Mission District in San Francisco." *Faculty – Arts and Social Change* (New College of California, 1991).

Moline, Mary. *Norman Rockwell Encyclopedia: A Chronological Catalog of the Artist's Work 1910–1978.* Indianapolis: Curtis Publishing Company.

Morelia, Joe, Edward Epstein, and Eleanor Clark. *Those Great Movie Ads.* New Rochelle, N.Y.: Arlington House, 1972.

Morse, John D., ed. *Ben Shahn.* New York: Praeger Publishers, 1972.

Mouse, Stanley, and Alton Kelley. *Mouse and Kelley.* New York: Dragon's World/Dell, 1979.

Muller-Brockmann, Josef, and Shizuko Muller-Brockman. *History of the Poster.* Zurich: ABC Editions, 1971.

Murgatroyd, Keith. *Modern Graphics.* London: Studio Vista, 1974.

Neill, Alex. "At War over Rock Posters," *Marin Independent-Journal* (San Rafael, Calif.), 23 Feb. 1987.

Nolan, Dennis. "The Rock and Roll Poster Phenomenon" (unpublished paper, San Jose State University, California, 1968).

O'Connor, Francis, comp. *Art for the Millions: Essays by Artists and Administrators of the WPA Federal Art Project*. Greenwich, Conn.: New York Graphic Society, 1979.

Paintings by Jerry Ingram. Anadarko, Oklahoma: Southern Plains Indian Museum and Crafts Center, 1982.

Paret, Peter, Beth Irwin Lewis, and Paul Paret. *Persuasive Images: Posters of War and Revolution from the Hoover Institution Archives*. New Jersey: Princeton University Press, 1992.

Penfield, Edward. *Posters in Miniature*. New York: R. H. Russell & Son, 1896.

Pennell, Joseph. *Joseph Pennell's Liberty-Loan Poster: A Textbook for Artists and Amateurs, Governments and Printers*. Philadelphia: J. B. Lippincott, 1918.

"Personalities: 'Murphy' and Rick Griffin," *Surfer* 3, no. 3 (Aug./Sept. 1962).

"Peter Gee Lends Talent to Library Exhibit Poster." *Library of Congress Information Bulletin* 33, no. 34 (23 Aug. 1974): 281–86.

Peter Max: A Retrospective. The Eastern European Museum Tour. New York: Optimum Graphics, 1991.

Peterson, Clark. "A Hep Cat Named Mouse." *Relix* 8, no. 4 (Aug. 1981).

———. "It's David Singer, Not the Song." *Relix* 8, no. 4 (Aug. 1981).

Pheifer, Pat. "Robert Connolly 77; was longtime artist in Twin Cities," *Minneapolis Star Tribune*, 2 June 1995.

Platt, John. "Rick Griffin: A Life of Art . . . And the Art of Life." *Zig-Zag* (c. 1971).

———. "Notes on Kelley and Mouse; Quicksilver Family Tree," *Comstock Lode* 7 (spring 1980).

"Pop! Goes the Poster: Pop Art Portraits of Comic Book Favorites," *Newsweek*, 29 March 1965.

Poster Art of the World. Exh. cat. Toronto: Royal Ontario Museum/University of Toronto Press, 1960.

Prescott, Kenneth W. *The Complete Graphic Works of Ben Shahn*. New York: Quadrangle/New York Times Book Company, 1973.

———. *Prints and Posters of Ben Shahn*. New York: Dover Publications, Inc., 1982.

Price, Charles Matlack. *Poster Design*. Rev. ed. New York: George W. Bricka, 1922.

"Printing . . . A Craft with Posterity in Mind,"

Independent & Gazette (Berkeley), 6 Apr. 1980.

Progner, Jean, and Patricia Dreyfus. "The Poster Revolution: Artifact into Art." *Print*, (July–Aug. 1971).

"Psychedelic Revival." *Relix* 14, no. 1 (Feb. 1987).

Purvis, Tom. *Poster Progress*. Edited by F. A. Mercer and W. Gaunt. London and New York: The Studio, c. 1938.

Rand, Paul. *Thoughts on Design*. New York: Wittenborn, Schultz Inc., 1951.

Rawls, Walton. *Wake Up, America!*. New York: Abbeville Press, Inc., 1988.

Read, R. B. "These are the Boys that Made the Art that Sparked the Scene . . ." *California Living*, 20 Nov. 1966.

Reade, Brian. *Aubrey Beardsley*. New York: Viking Press, 1967.

Reed, Walt, and Roger Reed. *The Illustrator in America 1880–1980: A Century of Illustration*. New York: The Society of Illustrators, 1984.

Rennert, Jack. *100 Posters of Buffalo Bill's Wild West*. New York: Harper & Row, 1973.

———. *100 Years of Bicycle Posters*. New York: Harper & Row, 1973.

———. *100 Years of Circus Posters*. New York: Avon Books, 1974.

———. *Poster Classics*. New York: Phillips, 1980.

———. *19th and 20th Century Posters*. New York: Phillips, 1981.

———. *100 Poster Masterpieces*. New York: Phillips, 1981.

———. *Poster Extravaganza*. New York: Poster Auctions International, Inc., 1992.

———. *Winning Posters*. New York: Poster Auctions International, Inc., 1994.

Retrospective Tony Palladino 1952–1985. Exh. cat. New York: School of Visual Arts Press, Ltd., 1985.

Revolution from the Hoover Institution Archives. New Jersey: Princeton University Press, 1992.

Reynolds, Charles, and Regina Reynolds. *100 Years of Magic Posters*. New York: Grosset & Dunlap, 1976.

Richmond, Leonard, ed. *The Technique of the Poster*. London: Isaac Pitman & Sons, 1933.

Rickards, Maurice. *Posters of the First World War*. New York: Walker & Company, 1968.

———. *Posters of the Nineteen Twenties*. New York:

Walker & Company, 1968.

———. *Banned Posters*. London: Evelyn Adams & Mackay, 1969.

———. *The Rise and Fall of the Poster*. New York: McGraw-Hill, 1971.

Rickards, Maurice, and Michael Moody. *The First World War: Ephemera, Mementos and Documents*. London: Jupiter Books, 1975.

Robinson, Roxana. *Georgia O'Keeffe: A Life*. New York: Harper & Row, 1989.

Rossi, Attilio. *Posters*. London: Paul H mlyn, 1966.

Rupert García. Exh. cat. San Francisco: Harcourts Gallery, 1985.

Rupert García: Prints and Posters: 1967–1990. Exh. cat. San Francisco: The Fine Arts Museums of San Francisco, 1990.

Salberg, Lester S. "The San Francisco Psychedelic Dance Posters" (unpublished paper, University of California, Berkeley, 1969).

Schapiro, Steve, and David Chierichetti. *The Movie Poster Book*. New York: E. P. Dutton, 1979.

Selz, Peter. "The Hippie Poster." *Graphis* (1968).

Serwer, Jacqueline Days. "The American Poster of the 1890s" (Ph.D. diss., City University of New York, 1980).

Shelton, Cyril. *A History of Poster Advertising*. London: Chapman & Hall, 1937.

Simmons, Jan. *Bill Graham Enterprises & An Abbreviated History of Bill Graham Presents*. San Francisco: Bill Graham Presents, c. 1986.

Simmons, Jan, Rita Gentry-Turrmi, and Dennis McNally. *Bill Graham Presents: 11 Years of Rock & Roll (1965–1976), Taken from His Calendars*. San Francisco: Bill Graham Presents, c. 1976.

Sloan, John. *American Art Noveau: The Poster Period of John Sloan*. Compiled by Helen Farr Sloan. Lockhaven, Pa: Privately published by Hammermill Paper Company, Lock Haven Division, 1967.

Stanley, Eliot H. "The Lively Poster Arts of Rockwell Kent," *Journal of Decorative and Propaganda Arts, 1875–1945* (spring 1989): 6–31.

Stenner, Dugald. "Rock Posters," *Journal of Communications* 9 (Sept. 1967).

———. *The Art of Revolution: 96 Posters from Castro's Cuba, 1959–1970*. New York: McGraw-Hill, 1970.

Stevens, Carol. "A Passionate Response," *Print* 46 (May–June 1992): 56–65, 120.

Territo, Joseph. "Alton Kelley: Spirit of the Sixties." *Relix* 8, no. 4 (Aug. 1981).

Terry, Walter. *100 Years of Dance Posters*. New York: Darien House, c. 1975.

Theoriles, George. *America, Posters of World War I*. New York: Dafran House, 1973.

U.S. World War I Posters from the Collection of the Smithsonian Institution's Division of Political History. Washington, D. C.: Smithsonian Institution, n.d.

Walker, Cummings G., ed. *The Great Poster Trip: Art Eureka*. Palo Alto, Calif.: Coyne & Blanchard, 1968.

Weber, Jeff. "60s Poster Artist [Stanley Mouse] Opens Local Studio," *Argus-Courier* (Petaluma, Calif.), 26 Nov. 1982.

Weill, Alain. *The Poster: A Worldwide Survey and History*. Boston: G. K. Hall, 1985.

Weitenkampf, Frank. *American Graphic Art*. New York: Henry Holt, 1912.

"Wes Wilson: Top Dog of the Poster Rage," *California Living*, 20 Nov. 1966.

Wilson, Ma Lin. "An American Phenomenon: On Marketing Georgia O'Keeffe." *From the Faraway Nearby: Georgia O'Keeffe as Icon*. Christopher Merrill and Ellen Bradbury, eds. Reading, Mass.: Addison-Wesley Publishing Company, 1992.

Wong, Roberta Waddell. *American Posters of the Nineties*. Exh. cat. Boston: Boston Public Library, 1974.

World War I Propaganda Posters, A Selection from the Bowman Gray Collection. Chapel Hill: Ackland Art Center, University of North Carolina, 1969.

Wrede, Stuart. *The Modern Poster*. Exh. cat. New York: Museum of Modern Art, 1988.

Wye, Deborah. *Committed to Print: Social and Political Themes in Recent American Art*. New York: Museum of Modern Art, 1988.

Yanker, Gary. *Prop Art*. New York: Darien House, 1972.

Zeman, Zbynek. *Art and Propaganda in World War II*. London: Orbis, 1978.

Chronological Index

1895 William H. Bradley, Narcoti Chemical Co. (Springfield, Mass.), *Narcoti-Cure*, plate 33.

1895 William H. Bradley, Stone & Kimball (Chicago), *The Chap-Book: Thanksgiving Number*, plate 32.

1895 Maynard Dixon, *Overland*, plate 34.

1895 Arthur Wesley Dow, Louis Prang & Co. (Boston), *Modern Art*, plate 35.

1895 Florence Lundborg, William Doxey (San Francisco), *The Lark (November, 1895)*, plate 36.

1895 Ethel Reed, Lamson, Wolffe & Co. (Boston), printed by Heliotype Printing Co. (Boston), *Folly or Saintliness*, plate 38.

1895 Louis John Rhead, *The New York Sun, Read The Sun*, plate 37.

c. 1895 Charles Arthur Cox, *Bearings Magazine* (Chicago), *Bearings*, plate 46.

1896 William H. Bradley, The Overman Wheel Co. (Chicopee Falls, Mass.), *Victor Bicycles*, plate 41.

1896 Edward Penfield, Harper & Brothers (New York), *Harper's June*, plate 42.

1896 Edward Penfield, Stearns Manufacturing Company, *Ride a Stearns and Be Content*, plate 43.

1896 Edward Penfield, Harper & Brothers (New York), *Three Gringos*, plate 39.

1896 John Sloan, Copeland and Day (Boston), *Cinder-Path Tales*, plate 45.

1896 John Henry Twachtman, Stone & Kimball (New York), *The Damnation of Theron Ware (or Illumination)*, plate 40.

c. 1896 Edward Penfield, Waltham Manufacturing Co. (New York), *Orient Cycles*, plate 44.

1897 Maxfield Parrish, *The Adlake Camera*, plate 47.

1897 Maxfield Parrish, The Century Co. (New York), printed by The Thomas & Wylie Lithographic Co., *The Century Midsummer Holiday Number*, plate 49.

1897 Maxfield Parrish, Harper & Brothers (New York), *Harper's Weekly*, plate 48.

1899 Frederick Winthrop Ramsdell, *American Crescent Cycles*, plate 50.

c. 1900 Unknown, International Stock Food Co., *Do You Want More Milk? Feed Your Cows International Stock Food*, plate 51.

1903 Bristow Adams, Potomac Press, Washington, D.C., *Mercersburg*, plate 116.

1907 Unknown, Strobridge Lithographing Company, *The Barnum & Bailey Greatest Show on Earth: Ski Sailing*, plate 1.

1907 Unknown, Strobridge Lithographing Company, *Charles Frohman Presents Peter Pan*, plate 4.

1913 Unknown, Strobridge Lithographing Company, *The Barnum & Bailey Greatest Show on Earth: Mooney's "Giants,"* plate 2.

1915 Fred Spear, *Enlist*, plate 59.

1917 James Montgomery Flagg, *I Want You for U.S. Army*, plate 60.

c. 1917 Joseph Pennell, *That Liberty Shall Not Perish from the Earth – Buy Liberty Bonds*, plate 61.

1917–18 Charles Dana Gibson, *Help Her Carry On! "Miss America Reports for Service, Sir,"* plate 62.

1917–18 Edward Penfield, Y.W.C.A., *The Girl on the Land Serves the Nation's Need*, plate 63.

1918 Charles Livingston Bull, U.S. Food Administration, *Save the Products of the Land: Eat More Fish – They Feed Themselves*, plate 65.

1918 Howard Chandler Christy, *If You Want to Fight! Join the Marines*, plate 64.

1924 Unknown, Strobridge Lithographing Company, *Ringling Brothers and Barnum & Bailey Combined Shows: Seals That Exhibit Intelligence*, plate 3.

1926 Otto Brennemann, Chicago Lithography Company for the South Shore and South Bend Railroad, *Football: Notre Dame (South Bend)*, plate 117.

1928 Norman Erickson, William R. Crawford Lithography, *The Steel Mills at Gary by South Shore Line*, plate 52.

1933 Unknown, *Joseph M. Schenck Presents Walt Disney's Mickey Mouse in "Ye Olden Days,"* plate 5.

1936 Carken, Federal Art Project (Chicago), *Brookfield Zoo*, plate 6.

1936–41 Jack Rivolta, WPA, New York Federal Art

Project, *Up Where Winter Calls to Play,* plate 53.

1937 Lester Beall, *Light* from the "Rural Electrification Administration" series, plate 89.

1939 Joseph Binder, *New York World's Fair 1939,* plate 8.

1939 Paul Rand, *Dancer,* plate 7.

1939 Louis B. Siegriest, *Eskimo Mask . . . Western Alaska,* plate 90.

1941 Albert M. Bender, Federal Art Project (Chicago), *Jobs for Girls & Women,* plate 91.

1942 Jean Carlu, Division of Information, Office for Emergency Management (Washington, D.C.), *America's Answer! Production,* plate 66.

1942 Karl Koehler and Victor Ancona, *This Is the Enemy,* plate 67.

1942 Fred G. Korth, *Where Every Boy Can Dream of Being President,* from the series "This Is America," plate 94.

1942 Dorothea Lange, *Where a Fellow Can Start on the Home Team and Wind Up in the Big League,* from the series "This Is America," plate 95.

1942 Lawrence B. Smith, *Don't Let That Shadow Touch Them,* plate 69.

1942 Unknown, General Cable Corporation, *Are You Doing All You Can?,* plate 70.

c. 1942 J. Howard Miller, Westinghouse for War Production Coordinating Committee, *We Can Do It!,* plate 68.

c. 1942 Unknown, *If You Don't Need It . . . Don't Buy It!,* plate 93.

c. 1942 Unknown, *She's Helping . . . What Are You Doing?,* plate 92.

c. 1942 Unknown, *Women in Industry . . . We Can't Win without Them,* plate 71.

1943 Norman Rockwell, *Save Freedom of Speech,* plate 96.

1946 Ben Shahn, CIO Political Action Committee, *Break Reaction's Grip – Register – Vote,* plate 73.

1947 Erik Nitsche, New York Subway Association, *Say it Fast. . . Often. . . in Color,* plate 98.

1948 Ben Shahn, The Progressive Party (New York), *A Good Man Is Hard to Find: Truman and Dewey,* plate 72.

1949 Rockwell Kent, *Save This Right Hand,* plate 74.

1953 Unidentified, *Marilyn Monroe and "Niagara,"* plate 9.

1958 Saul Bass, *Vertigo,* plate 10.

1966 Stanley Mouse, *Grateful Dead, Oxford Circle (Avalon Ballroom),* plate 11

1966 Wes Wilson, West Coast Lithograph Co. (San Francisco), *Bill Graham Presents . . . Captain Beefhart and His Magic Band, Chocolate Watch Band, Fillmore Auditorium,* plate 12.

1966 Wes Wilson, Bill Graham Presents, *Presented in Dance-Concert by Bill Graham: Jefferson Airplane,* plate 13.

1967 Seymour Chwast, Push Pin Studios, *End Bad Breath,* plate 75.

1967 Bob Fried, *Charlatans: The Youngbloods and the Other Half,* plate 16.

1967 Rick Griffin, Family Dog Publishing, *Charlatans: The Salvation Army Banned Blue Cheer,* plate 14.

1967 Rick Griffin, *Charlatans: The 13th Floor Elevators,* plate 15.

1967 Victor Moscoso, Neon Rose, *Big Brother and the Holding Company,* plate 17.

1967 Victor Moscoso, Neon Rose, *The Chambers Brothers,* plate 18.

1967 Victor Moscoso, Neon Rose, *Sopwith Camel,* plate 19.

1967 James D. Rose, *The Last Redwoods – Sierra Club,* plate 99.

1967 William Taubin (art director) and Howard Zieff (photographer), *You Don't Have to Be Jewish to Love Levy's,* plate 54.

1967 Tomi Ungerer, *Black Power/White Power,* plate 100.

1968 Peter Gee, *Martin Luther King, Jr.,* plate 76.

1968 Victor Moscoso and Rick Griffin, *Bill Graham Presents in San Francisco: Jimi Hendrix Experience,* plate 20.

1968 Ben Shahn, Container Corporation of America, *You Have Not Converted a Man Because You Have Silenced Him,* plate 97.

c. 1968 Unknown, *Girls Say Yes to Boys Who Say No,* plate 77.

1969 Richard Avedon, Student Mobilization Committee to End the War in Vietnam (New York), *Who Has a Better Right to Oppose the War?,* plate 78.

1969 Rupert García, *No More o' This Shit,* plate 83.

1969 Peter Max, *From the Moon,* plate 21.

1969 Tomi Ungerer, The Electric Circus (New York), *The Electric Circus – The Ultimate Legal Entertainment Experience,* plate 101.

1970 Ron Borowski (photographer), Starfish Publications, *I Pledge Allegiance,* plate 82.

1970 R. L. Haeberle (photographer) and Peter Brandt (designer), Art Workers Coalition, *Q: And Babies? A: And Babies*, plate 79.

1970 Felice Regan, The Graphic Workshop, *Can You Spare a Pint of Blood for Peace?*, plate 102.

1970 Unknown, The Committee to Defend the Panther 21, *Power to the People*, plate 80.

1971 Roy Lichtenstein, H. K. L. Ltd. (New York and Boston), *Save Our Planet, Save Our Water*, plate 103.

1971 Georgia O'Keeffe, *Save Our Planet, Save Our Air*, plate 104.

1971 David Singer, *Bill Graham Presents in San Francisco: Fillmore West – Closing Week . . . June 30–July 4, 1971*, plate 22.

1972 J. Gokey, *This Is How the White Man's Law Fits the Indian*, plate 84.

1973 Xavier Viramontes, Printed by striking farmworkers, *Boycott Grapes: Support the United Farm Workers Union*, plate 85.

1974 Ivan Chermayeff, Department of the Interior, National Park Service, *Visit the American Museum of Immigration at the Statue of Liberty*, plate 81.

1974 Alice Neel, U.S. Olympic Committee, Kennedy Graphics, Inc. (New York), *Olympics 1976*, plate 118.

c. 1974 Lisa Emmons, New York Mobilization for Survival, *And Then There Was Nothing*, plate 88.

1975 Rupert García, *Inaugural Exhibit of Mexican and Chicano Art*, plate 23.

1975 Unknown, Women's Graphic Collective, *Passivity is the Dragon*, plate 107.

1976 Romare Bearden, Three Rivers Press, Carnegie Mellon University, *Africa Speaks to the West*, plate 105.

1976 Paul Davis, *For Colored Girls*, plate 24.

1977 Robert Connolly, *What You Take to the Lake . . . Take It Back!*, plate 106.

1978 Tony Palladino (designer) and Silas H. Rhodes (art director), School of Visual Arts (New York), *Having a Talent Isn't Worth Much Unless You Know What to Do with It*, plate 108.

1978 Larry Rivers, Circle Gallery (New York), *Madama Butterfly – Metropolitan Opera*, plate 25.

1979 Leonard Baskin, Printed by the Government Printing Office for the National Park Service, *Sitting Bull: Custer Battlefield* (renamed Little Bighorn Battlefield National Monument), plate 109.

1980 Patrick Nagel, Mirage Editions (Santa Monica), *The Paper Mill, Los Angeles*, plate 26.

1981 Karen Nicole Martin, Pro Creations Publishing Company (New Orleans), *1981 Boston Marathon*, plate 119.

1982 Stephen Frykholm, U.S. Ocean Promotion, *National Offshore Powerboat, 1982 Racing Circuit*, plate 120.

1982 Ester Hernandez, *Sun Mad Raisins*, plate 87.

1982 Lance Hidy, *Meriden-Stinehour*, plate 55.

1982 Robert Rauschenberg, Lincoln Center Film Society (New York), *20th New York Film Festival*, plate 27.

1982 Felice Regan, The Graphic Workshop, *Giant Panda*, plate 110.

1982 Raymond Saunders, Knapp Communications Corporation (Los Angeles), *Los Angeles 1984 Olympic Games*, plate 121.

1985 David Lance Goines, Student Health Service, University of California (Berkeley), *Aids Prevention*, plate 111.

1989 Guerrilla Girls, *Do Women Have to Be Naked to Get into The Metropolitan Museum?*, plate 86.

1990 Jerry Ingram, *Listen to the Drum: Name Your Tribe. Answer the Census*, plate 112.

1992 David Lance Goines, *Chez Panisse Café & Restaurant, Twenty-First Birthday*, plate 57.

1992 April Greiman, *Pikes Peak Lithographing Co.*, plate 56.

1993 Old City Group (designer) and Jim Erickson (photographer), National Postal Museum, Smithsonian Institution, *The National Postal Museum Opens July 30th*, plate 28.

1993 David Lance Goines, *Berkeley Conference Center & Visitors Bureau (Howl)*, plate 29.

1993 Doug Minkler, *Get a Life, Get a Bike*, plate 113.

1994 Art Chantry, *Kustom Kulture*, plate 30.

1994 Frank Kozik, Sneakyville Printing, *Nine Inch Nails*, plate 31.

1994 Robert Pisano and Randy O'Brezar (photographers), *Boeing 777*, plate 58.

1995 Milton Glaser, *Earth Fair (Art Air)*, plate 114.

1995 Jennifer Morla, Morla Design, Inc. (San Francisco), *Save Our Earth*, plate 115.

Index

Italic page numbers refer to illustrations.

Adams, Bristow, *152*
Adlake Camera, The (Parrish), *84*
Africa Speaks to the West (Bearden), *140*
Aids Prevention (Goines), *145*
Albers, Josef, 19, 169
American Crescent Cycles (Ramsdell), *87*
America's Answer! Production (Carlu), 22; *104*
Ancona, Victor, 22, 167; *105*
And Then There Was Nothing (Emmons), *123*
Anti-Cigarette League, 71
ApoGee Gallery, *164*
Are You Doing All You Can?, *109*
Art Nouveau, 161, 163, 165, 170, 172; *70*
Arts and Crafts movement, 168
Art Workers Coalition, *116*
Avalon Ballroom, 166, 169, 175; *47*
Avedon, Richard, 159; *115*

Baez, Joan, *114*
Balter, Frances, *140*
Barnet, Will, 177
Barnum & Bailey, 7, 161; *36, 37*
Barnum & Bailey Greatest Show on Earth: Mooney's "Giants," The, *36*
Barnum & Bailey Greatest Show on Earth: Ski Sailing, The, *36*
Barnum and Forepaugh posters, 28
Baskin, Leonard, 159; *143*
Bass, Saul, 160; *45*
Bass, Saul, and Associates, 160
Bauhaus posters, 22, 162, 165, 177
Bayer, Herbert, 165
Beall, Lester, 160; *126*
Bearden, Romare, 160; *140*
Beardsley, Aubrey, 161, 174
Bearings (Cox), *83*
Bearings Magazine, *83*
Bender, Albert M., 176; *128*
Berkeley Bonaparte, 166
Berkeley Conference Center & Visitors Bureau (Howl) (Goines), *64*
Big Brother and the Holding Company (Moscoso), *52*
Bill Graham Presents, 49, 55
Bill Graham Presents. . . Captain Beefhart & His Magic Band, Chocolate Watch

Band, Fillmore Auditorium (Wilson), *48*
Bill Graham Presents in San Francisco: Fillmore West – Closing Week. . . June 30–July 4, 1971 (Singer), *57*
Bill Graham Presents in San Francisco: Jimi Hendrix Experience (Moscoso and Griffin), *55*
Binder, Joseph, 22, 160–61; *42*
Black Power/White Power (Ungerer), *136*
Blue Rose (Mouse and Kelley), 169
Boeing 777 (Pisano and O'Brezar), *95*
Borowski, Ron, *119*
Boycott Grapes: Support the United Farm Workers Union (Viramontes), 175; *121*
Bradley, William H., 17–18, 28, 70, 71, 161, 171; *70, 79*
Bradley: His Chap-Book (Bradley), 17, 161, 170; *70*
Brandt, Peter, *116*
Break Reaction's Grip – Register – Vote (Shahn), 22; *111*
Brennemann, Otto, *153*
Bridges, Harry, *111*
Brookfield Zoo (Carken), *40*
Bull, Charles Livingston, 161; *103*
Bureau of the Census, 20, 21, *147*

Cahill, Holger, 177
Can You Spare a Pint of Blood for Peace? (Regan), *137*
Carken, 176; *40*
Carlu, Jean, 22, 161; *104*
Century Co., The, *86*
Century Midsummer Holiday Number, The (Parrish), *86*
Chambers Brothers, The (Moscoso), 19; *53*
Chantry, Art, 19, 161–62; *65*
Chap-Book: Thanksgiving Number, The (Bradley), *70*
Charlatans: The Salvation Army Banned Blue Cheer (Griffin), *50*
Charlatans: The 13th Floor Elevators (Griffin), *50*
Charlatans: The Youngbloods and the Other Half (Fried), *51*
Charles Frohman Presents Peter Pan, *38*
Chavez, Cesar, 163, 166
Chéret, Jules, 170; *80*

Chermayeff, Ivan, 2, 162; *118*
Chez Panisse Café & Restaurant, Twenty-First Birthday (Goines), 29; *94*
Chicago Lithography Company, *153*
Christy, Howard Chandler, 162; *102*
Chwast, Seymour, 162–63, 165; *112*
Cinder-Path Tales (Sloan), *82*
CIO Political Action Committee, *111*
Circle Gallery, *61*
circus posters, 7, 14, 22; *36, 37*
color lithography, 28, 33
Committee to Defend the Panther 21, The, *117*
Connolly, Robert, 163; *141*
Container Corporation of America, *133*
Copeland and Day, *82*
Coughlin, Father, *105*
Cox, Charles Arthur, *83*
Crawford, William R., Lithography, *89*
Creel, George, 25
Curtis Publishing, 25

Damnation of Theron Ware (or Illumination), The (Twachtman), *78*
Dancer (Rand), 29; *41*
Davis, Paul, 163; *60*
Davis, Stuart, 177
Department of the Interior, National Park Service, *118, 143*
digital printmaking, 28, 33
Disney, Walt, 39
Division of Information, Office for Emergency Management, *104*
Division of Pictorial Publicity, Federal Committee of Public Information, 25, 165, 171; *103*
Dixon, Maynard, 163; *72*
Don't Let That Shadow Touch Them (Smith), *108*
Dorfsman, Louis, *119*
dot screen, 26
Dow, Arthur Wesley, 163, 170; *73*
Do Women Have to Be Naked to Get into the Metropolitan Museum? (Guerrilla Girls), *122*
Doxey, William, *74*
Do You Want More Milk? Feed Your Cows International Stock Food, *88*

Earth Fair (Art Air) (Glaser), *148*
Electric Circus, The, *137*

Electric Circus – The Ultimate Legal Entertainment Experience, The (Ungerer), *137*
Emmons, Lisa, *123*
End Bad Breath (Chwast), *112*
Enlist (Spear), 17; *16, 17, 98*
Erickson, Jim, *63*
Erickson, Norman, *89*
Eskimo Mask. . .Western Alaska (Siegriest), *127*
exhibition posters, 19

Family Dog Publishing, 166, 169; *50*
Farm Security Administration, 168, 173
Federal Art Project. *See under* Works Progress Administration
Federal Committee of Public Information, Division of Pictorial Publicity of, 25, 165, 171; *103*
Fillmore Auditorium, 174, 175; *48, 54, 57*
film posters, 19; *44–45*
Flagg, James Montgomery, 14, 23, 163–64; *99*
Floethe, Richard, 177
Folly or Saintliness (Reed), *75*
Football: Notre Dame (South Bend) (Brennemann), *153*
For Colored Girls (Davis), *60*
Four Freedoms (Rockwell), 7, 23, 25; *24, 25, 132*
Fried, Bob, *51*
From the Moon (Max), *56*
Frykholm, Stephen, 164; *156*

Galeria de la Raza, 175
García, Rupert, 14, 17, 164, 166; *59, 119*
Gaston, Lucy Page, *71*
Gauguin, Paul, *77*
Gee, Peter, 164; *29, 30–31, 113*
Gehenna Press, 159
Geismer, Tom, 162
General Cable Corporation, *109*
German posters, 22
Get a Life, Get a Bike (Minkler), *148*
Giant Panda (Regan), *144*
Gibson, Charles Dana, 25, 164–65, 171; *100*
"Gibson girl," 165
Ginsberg, Alan, 64
Girl on the Land Serves the Nation's Need, The (Penfield), *101*
Girls Say Yes to Boys Who Say No, 20; *114*
Glaser, Milton, 164, 165; *148*
Godine Press, 166–67
Goines, David Lance, 29, 165; *64, 94, 145*
Gokey, J., *120*

Golden Gate International Exposition, *127*
Good Man Is Hard to Find (depicting Truman and Dewey), *A* (Shahn), 14, 22; *14, 15, 110*
Government Printing Office, *143*
Graham, Bill, 18, 19, 174, 175
Graphic Workshop, 172; *137, 144*
Grateful Dead, The, 166; *47*
Grateful Dead, Oxford Circle (Avalon Ballroom) (Mouse), *47*
"Great Ideas of Western Man" series, *133*
Greiman, April, 165–66; *92–93*
Griffin, Rick, 19, 166; *50, 51, 55*
Grosz, George, 160, 171, 175
Guerrilla Girls, 122
Guerrilla Girls West, 122

Haeberle, R. L., *116*
Harding, Richard, 17
Harper & Brothers, 17; *77, 80, 85*
Harper's, 170, 171; *80*
Harper's June (Penfield), *80*
Harper's Weekly (Parrish), *85*
Having a Talent Isn't Worth Much Unless You Know What to Do with It (Palladino and Rhodes), *142*
Hearst, William Randolph, *105*
Heimann, Jim, 177
Helms, Chet, 166
Help Her Carry On! "Miss America Reports for Service, Sir" (Gibson), *100*
Hernandez, Ester, 166; *123*
Hidy, Lance, 166–67; *91*
H. K. L. Ltd., *138, 139*
Howl, 64

If You Don't Need It . . . Don't Buy It!, *129*
If You Want to Fight! Join the Marines (Christy), *102*
Inaugural Exhibit of Mexican and Chicano Art (García), 14; *59*
Ingram, Jerry, 167; *20, 21, 147*
Institute of American Indian Arts, 20; *21, 147*
International Stock Food Co., *88*
I Pledge Allegiance (Borowski), *119*
Irvine, William Mann, *152*
I Want You for U.S. Army (Flagg), 7, 14, 23, 164; *99*

Jobs for Girls & Women (Bender), *128*
Joseph M. Schenck Presents Walt Disney's Mickey Mouse in "Ye Olden Days," *39*
"Jugendstil and Expressionism" (University of California at Berkeley), 18

Kahlo, Frida, 14, 164
Kelley, Alton, 169; *51*
Kennedy Graphics, *154*
Kent, Rockwell, 167; *111*
Kepes, Gyorgy, 160
King, Martin Luther, Jr., 29; *30–31, 113*
Knapp Communications Corporation, *157*
Koehler, Karl, 22, 167; *105*
Korth, Fred G., *130*
Kozik, Frank, 167; *67*
Krasner, Lee, 177
Kustom Kulture (Chantry), 19; *65*

Lake Minnetonka Conservation District, *141*
Lamson, Wolffe & Co., *75*
Lange, Dorothea, 163, 167–68; *131*
Lark, The, 168; *74*
Lark (November, 1895), The (Lundborg), *74*
Last Redwoods – Sierra Club, The (Rose), *135*
letterpress, 33
Lichtenstein, Roy, 26, 29, 168; *138*
Light (Beall), *126*
Lincoln Center Film Society, 62
Listen to the Drum: Name Your Tribe. Answer the Census (Ingram), 20; *20, 21, 147*
literary posters, 13, 22; *74–75, 77–78, 80*
lithography, 26
Los Angeles 1984 Olympic Games (Saunders), *157*
Lundborg, Florence, 168; *74*
Lusitania, 17; *16, 17, 98*

MacLeish, Archibald, 22, 23
Madama Butterfly – Metropolitan Opera (Rivers), *61*
Marilyn Monroe and "Niagara," 20; *44*
Martin, Karen Nicole, *155*
Martin Luther King, Jr. (Gee), 29; *30–31, 113*
Max, Peter, 28, 168; *56*
Mercersburg (Adams), *152*
Meriden-Stinehour (Hidy), *91*
Miller, J. Howard, 12, 13, *106*
Minkler, Doug, 168–69; *148*
Mirage Editions, *61*
Modern Art (Dow), *73*
Monroe, Marilyn, 20; *44*
Morla, Jennifer, *149*
Morla Design, Inc., *149*
Morley, John Viscount, *133*
Moscoso, Victor, 19, 169; *52, 53, 54, 55*
Mouse, Stanley, 19, 169; *47, 51*
Mouse Studios, 169

Nagel, Patrick, 169; 61
Narcoti Chemical Co., 17–18; 71
Narcoti-Cure (Bradley), 17–18; 71
National Offshore Powerboat, 1982
    Racing Circuit (Frykholm), 156
National Park Service, 118, 143
National Postal Museum Opens July 30th
    (Old City Group and Erickson), 63
National Postal Museum, Smithsonian
    Institution, 63
National Youth Association, 128
Neel, Alice, 169; 154
Neon Rose, 169; 52, 53, 54
New Deal, 176. *See also under* Works
    Progress Administration
New York Mobilization for Survival, 123
New York Subway Association, 134
New York World's Fair 1939 (Binder), 22;
    42
Nine Inch Nails (Kozik), 20; 67
1981 Boston Marathon (Martin), 155
Nitsche, Erik, 169–70; 134
No More o' This Shit (García), 14, 17; 119

O'Brezar, Randy, 95
Office for Emergency Management,
    Division of Information, 104
Office of War Information (OWI), 22,
    23, 174
offset lithography, 26, 28, 33
O'Keeffe, Georgia, 170; 139
Old City Group, 63
Olivetti Corporation, 139
Olympics 1976 (Neel), 154
"On the American Home Front"
    (Vanderbilt University Fine Arts
    Gallery), 22
Orient Cycles (Penfield), 26, 27, 81
outsider art, 161–62
Overland (Dixon), 72
Overman Wheel Co., The, 79
Oxendine, Tom, 20

Palladino, Tony, 170; 142
Paper Mill, Los Angeles, The (Nagel), 61
Parrish, Maxfield, 170; 84, 85, 86
Passion of Sacco and Vanzetti, The
    (Shahn), 111
Passivity Is the Dragon, 141
Penfield, Edward, 26, 28, 170–71; 26, 27,
    77, 80, 81, 101
Pennell, Joseph, 171; 100
photomechanical lithography, 28
photo-offset, 33
Pikes Peak Lithographing Co., The
    (Greiman), 92–93
Pisano, Robert, 95

"Poetry on the Buses," 140
Poetry on the Buses project, 160
Pollock, Jackson, 177
Pop art, 26, 164, 168, 173
Posters American Style (Chermayeff),
    2, 192
Potomac Press, 152
"Powers of Persuasion: Poster Art From
    World War II" (National Archives), 22
Power to the People, 117
Prang, Louis, & Co., 172; 73
*Presented in Dance-Concert by Bill
    Graham: Jefferson Airplane* (Wilson),
    49
Pro Creations Publishing Company, 155
Progressive Party, The, 14; 15, 110
propaganda posters, 22. *See also* World
    War I posters; World War II posters
protest posters, 20, 22, 168; 112–17,
    119–23, 136–39, 141, 149
Pushpin Group, The, 75, 148–49
Push Pin Press, 162
Push Pin Studios, 162–63, 164, 165

Q: And Babies? A: And Babies (Haeberle
    and Brandt), 116

Ramsdell, Frederick Winthrop, 171; 87
Rand, Paul, 29, 171; 41
Rauschenberg, Robert, 171–72; 62
Read The Sun, The (Rhead), 74
Reed, Ethel, 172; 75
Regan, Felice, 172; 137, 144
Remington, Frederic, 72
Rhead, Louis John, 172–73; 74
Rhodes, Silas H., 142
Ride a Stearns and Be Content (Penfield),
    81
*Ringling Brothers and Barnum & Bailey
    Combined Shows: Seals That Exhibit
    Intelligence*, 37
Rivers, Larry, 173; 61
Rivolta, Jack, 176; 90
rock posters, 18–19, 20, 22, 166, 167,
    169, 174; 47–55, 57, 65, 67
Rockwell, Norman, 7, 23, 25, 173; 24,
    25, 132
Rolling Stones, 174
Roosevelt, Franklin Delano, 23, 176; 105,
    126, 132
Rose, James D., 135
Royal Chicano Air Force (RCAF), 28
Rural Electrification Administration, 126
"Rural Electrification Administration"
    series, 126
Russell, 72
Russian Constructivists, 22, 177; 126

Saint Hieronymous Press, 165
San Francisco rock concerts, 47, 51–55, 57
Saturday Evening Post, 23, 173; 132
Saunders, Raymond Jennings, 173; 157
Save Freedom of Speech (Rockwell), 23,
    25; 24, 25, 132
Save Our Earth (Morla), 149
Save Our Planet, Save Our Air
    (O'Keeffe), 139
Save Our Planet, Save Our Water
    (Lichtenstein), 29; 138
*Save the Products of the Land: Eat More
    Fish–They Feed Themselves* (Bull), 103
Save This Right Hand (Kent), 111
Say it Fast. . .Often. . . in Color (Nitsche),
    134
School of Visual Arts, 142
Schwarz, Jordan A., 102
Seattle rock groups, 65
serigraphy, 33
Shahn, Ben, 14, 22, 173–74; 14, 15, 110,
    111, 133
She's Helping. . .What Are You Doing?,
    129
Siegriest, Louis B., 127
silkscreening, 33, 176
Singer, David, 174; 57
Sitting Bull: Custer Battlefield (Baskin),
    143
Sloan, John, 174; 82
Smith, Lawrence B., 108
Sneakyville Printing, 67
Society of Illustrators, 25, 165
Somervell, Brehon, 177
Sontag, Susan, 13
Sopwith Camel (Moscoso), 54
South Shore and South Bend Railroad, 153
Spear, Fred, 17; 16, 17, 98
Spiral, 160
sports posters, 152–57
Stanley, Eliot, 111
Starfish Publications, 119
Statue of Liberty, 100
Stearns Manufacturing Company, 81
Steel Mills at Gary by South Shore Line
    (Erickson), 89
Steinlen, 82
Stinehour, Roderick, 91
Stone & Kimball, 70, 78
Strobridge Lithographing Company, 14,
    28; 36, 37, 38
Student Health Service, University of
    California (Berkeley), 145
Student Mobilization Committee to End
    the War in Vietnam, 115
Sun Mad Raisins (Hernandez), 7, 20,
    166; 123

Taubin, William, 20; *91*
Taylor, Paul, 168; *131*
*That Liberty Shall Not Perish from the
    Earth – Buy Liberty Bonds* (Pennell),
    100
"This Is America," *130–31*
*This Is How the White Man's Law Fits
    the Indian* (Gokey), *120*
This Is Nazi Brutality (Shahn), *22*
This Is the Enemy (Koehler and Ancona),
    22, 167; *105*
Thomas & Wylie Lithographic Co.,
    The, *86*
Three Gringos (Penfield), *77*
Three Rivers Press (Carnegie Mellon
    University), *140*
Toulouse-Lautrec, Henri de, 170; *80*
Truman, Harry S., 14, 15, *110*
Twachtman, John Henry, 174–75; *78*
20th New York Film Festival
    (Rauschenberg), *62*
Twins, The (Bradley), *161*
Tyler Graphics, 168

Ungerer, Tomi, 175; *136, 137*
U.S. Food Administration, *103*
U.S. Ocean Promotion, *156*
U.S. Olympic Committee, *154*
University of California at Berkeley,
    18; *145*
Up Where Winter Calls to Play (Rivolta),
    90

Velonis, Anthony, 176
Vertigo, *45*
Victor Bicycles (Bradley), *79*
Viramontes, Xavier, 175; *121*
*Visit the American Museum of
    Immigration at the Statue of Liberty*
    (Chermayeff), *118*
Viva la Huelga (Davis), *163*

Waltham Manufacturing Co., *81*
Wayside Press, *161*
We Can Do It! (Miller), 12, 13, *106*
West Coast Lithograph Co., *48*
Westinghouse for War Production
    Coordinating Committee, 12, 13, *106*
*What You Take to the Lake. . .Take It
    Back!* (Connolly), 163; *141*
*Where a Fellow Can Start on the Home
    Team and Wind Up in the Big League*
    (Lange), *131*
*Where Every Boy Can Dream of Being
    President* (Korth), *130*
Whistler, James Abbott McNeill, *100*
*Who Has a Better Right to Oppose the
    War?* (Avedon), *115*
Wilson, Wes, 18–19, 28, 169, 175–76;
    48, 49
Winterland Arena, 169
*Women in Industry. . .We Can't Win with-
    out Them*, *109*
Women's Graphic Collective, *141*
woodblock, 26, 33
Works Progress Administration (WPA)
    Federal Art Project (FAP), Easel
    Division, 169
Works Progress Administration (WPA)
    Federal Art Project (FAP), Poster
    Division, 13, 22, 25, 176–77; *40, 90,
    127, 128*
Works Projects Administration, 176. *See
    also under* Works Progress
    Administration
World War I posters, 7, 14, 17, 22–23,
    25, 161, 162, 171; *16–17, 98–103*
World War II posters, 14, 22–23, 25, 167,
    174; *12, 13, 24, 25, 99, 104–6, 108–9,
    132*

Yañez, Rene, 175
*You Don't Have to Be Jewish to Love
    Levy's* (Taubin and Zieff), 20; *91*
*You Have Not Converted a Man Because
    You Have Silenced Him* (Shahn), *133*
Young Women's Christian Association
    (Y.W.C.A.), *101*

Zieff, Howard, 20; *91*

Credits

Photograph Credits

Published on the occasion of the exhibition "Posters American Style," organized by the National Museum of American Art, Smithsonian Institution

Exhibition Tour Schedule

National Museum of American Art, Washington, D.C.: March 27, 1998–August 9, 1998

Norton Museum of Art, West Palm Beach, Florida: August 29, 1998–October 25, 1998

The Santa Barbara Museum of Art: January 23, 1999–March 21, 1999

The Oakland Museum of California: June 12, 1999–August 15, 1999

Guest Curator: Therese Thau Heyman
Project Assistant: Jeana Foley

This book and the exhibition were made possible in part by generous gifts from Helen and Dr. Peter Bing

The National Museum of American Art, Smithsonian Institution, is dedicated to the preservation, exhibition, and study of the visual arts in America. The museum, whose publications program also includes the scholarly journal *American Art,* has extensive research resources: the database of the Inventories of American Painting and Sculpture, several image archives, and a variety of fellowships for scholars. The Renwick Gallery, one of the nation's premier craft museums, is part of NMAA. For more information or a catalogue of publications, write: Office of Publications, National Museum of American Art, MRC 230, Smithsonian Institution, Washington, D.C. 20560. NMAA also maintains a World Wide Web site at http://www.nmaa.si.edu

For Harry N. Abrams, Inc.:
Project Manager: Margaret L. Kaplan
Editor: Margaret E. Braver
Designer: E. Nygaard Ford

For National Museum of American Art:
Editors: Theresa Slowik and Janet Wilson

Library of Congress Cataloging-in-Publication Data

Heyman, Therese Thau.
    Posters American style / by Therese Thau Heyman.
        p.   cm.
    Accompanies an exhibition that opens at the National Museum of American Art, Washington, D.C. in the spring of 1998.
    "In association with Harry N. Abrams."
    Includes bibliographical references and indexes
    ISBN 0-8109-3749-2 (clothbound).
    ISBN 0-8109-2780-2 (mus. pbk.)
    1. Posters, American—Exhibitions. 2. Posters—19th century—United States—Exhibitions. 3. Posters—20th century—United States—Exhibitions.
    I. Title.
    NC1807.U5H49   1998
    741.6'44'0973074753—dc21   97-38050

Copyright © 1998 by the National Museum of American Art, Smithsonian Institution
Published in 1998 by Harry N. Abrams, Incorporated, New York, in association with the National Museum of American Art, Smithsonian Institution, Washington, D.C. All rights reserved. No part of the contents of this book may be reproduced without the written permission of the National Museum of American Art and the publisher

Printed and bound in Japan

Harry N. Abrams, Inc.
100 Fifth Avenue
New York, N.Y. 10011
www.abramsbooks.com

Frontispiece: Ivan Chermayeff. *Posters American Style.* 1997. Cut paper and assemblage, 29 x 22 in. (73.5 x 56 cm). Collection Ivan Chermayeff. Commissioned by the National Museum of American Art for the exhibition, "Posters American Style," in celebration of a century of American posters

American Style is a cha[p]
may have many meanings,
demonstrates. While rarit[y]
tant considerations in ma[ny]
by definition numerous a[n]
They reach out; they are
appear everywhere. Yet in
ety, they fulfill the one ov[er]
communicate effectively.
a complex layering of wo[rds]